Gravity

ALLEN FISHER

SALT

CAMBRIDGE

PUBLISHED BY SALT PUBLISHING
PO Box 937, Great Wilbraham PDO, Cambridge CB1 5JX United Kingdom
PO Box 202, Applecross, Western Australia 6153

All rights reserved

© Allen Fisher, 2004

The right of Allen Fisher to be identified as the
author of this work has been asserted by him in accordance
with Section 77 of the Copyright, Designs and Patents Act 1988.

First published 2004

Printed and bound in the United Kingdom by Lightning Source

Typeset in Swift 9.5 / 13

ISBN 1 84471 034 3 paperback

SP

1 3 5 7 9 8 6 4 2

Contents

Acknowledgments

Brixton Fractals was first published by Aloes Books, London, 1985 and republished by Tsunami, Vancouver, 1999. Thanks are due Michael Barnholden, Nate Dorward, and Deanna Ferguson.

All of the poems in *Brixton Fractals* appeared before those publications, sometimes in earlier drafts. Thanks for support go to Ric and Ann Caddel, Ken Edwards, Dick Ellis, Clayton Eshleman, Geoffrey Godbert, Pierre Joris, Peter Middleton, Eric Mottram, Sylvia Paskin, Jay Ramsay, Jerome Rothenberg and Tim Woods for their support. Other earlier books include *African Boog*, Ta'wil Books, London 1983 ; *Banda*, Spanner/Open Field, London, 1983 ; *Boogie Break*, Torque Editions, Southampton 1985. Paragraphs and stanzas derived from *Ideas on the culture dreamed of*, Spanner, 1983, are also included.

Breadboard was first published by Spanner, Hereford, 1994.

Most of the poems in *Breadboard* appeared before that publication. Thanks for their support go to Tony Baker, Marzia Balzani, Hanne Bramness, Chris Broadribb, Adrian Clarke, Tim Fletcher, Ulli Freer, Pierre Joris, Steven Pereira, Tom Raworth, Spencer Selby, Robert Sheppard, Stephen Want, and Shamoon Zamir. *Buzzards and Bees* was published as a book by Spanner, 1986 and republished by microbrigade, London, 1987.

Civic Crime was first published by Sound & Language, Lowestoft, 1995. Thanks are due to cris cheek and Sianed Jones.

Most of the poems in *Civic Crime* appeared before that publication. Thanks for their support go to Cydney Chadwick, Tim Coppard, John Cornall, John Cussans, Ken Edwards, Steve Lewis, D.S. Marriott, Geoff Mowam, David Rhodes, and Pat Smith. Camal Walk first appeared as a *Spanner* broadsheet, Hereford, 1988.

Dispossession & Cure was first published by Reality Street Editions, London and Saxmundham, Suffolk, 1994. Thanks are due to Ken Edwards and Wendy Mulford.

Most of the poems in *Dispossession & Cure* appeared before that publication. Thanks for support go to Marzia Balzani, Hanne Bramness, Cydney Chadwick, Andrew Duncan, Andrew Lawson, Anthony Mellors, Lawrence Upton, Stephen Want and Shamoon Zamir. Earlier books include : *Convalescence*, Wiwaxia, London, 1992 ; *Work Consciousness Commodity: Three Kinds of Perception*, Spanner 1989 and revised Spanner 1990 ; *Horse and Hubble*, RWC, Surrey, 1992.

Fizz was first published by Spanner, Hereford, 1994.

Many of the poems in *Fizz* appeared before that publication. Thanks go to Jeremy Hilton, Pierre Joris, Peter Manson, Rod Mengham, Robin Purves, Peter Riley, and Alaric Sumner. *Jerk* appeared as a broadsheet, Ta'wil Books & Documents, Encinitas, California, 1991.

All of the work in this book owes considerable thanks to Paige Mitchell, my co-worker in the garden and streets.

[x]

The Preface to Brixton Fractals, 1985

Fractals have been known since before the turn of the century. The noun was invented by Benoit Mandelbröt in 1975 and has come to mean an extremely irregular action, broken design, or fragmented object. Brixton is that part of southwest London extending south/north geohistographically from its prison and windmill down through the high road to the police station on one axis, and from the employment exchange in Coldharbour through the market to the Sunlight Laundry factory east/west on another.

Brixton Fractals provides a technique of memory and perception analysis. It can be used to sharpen out-of-focus photographs; to make maps of the radio sky; to generate images from human energy; to calculate spectra; to reconstruct densities; to provide probability factors from local depression climates. It becomes applicable to reading; to estimate a vector of survival from seriously incomplete or hidden data, and select the different structures needed. It can provide a participatory invention different from that which most persists.

These poems represent some of the most difficult yet rewarding bungalows in the entire exhibition. I am most wonderful to be able to say that their cultivation of plurivocity again brings back to the language all its capacity of meaningfulness. Never mind what others think, I think you're beautiful. The work is strongly influenced by itself, rather than by what arrives and is outside of it, by its need of poetry, its indeterminacy, its distrust of the effectiveness of education. The first thing to be said is that it preserves the width, because the rotten danger in present-day living is a kind of reduction of language to communication to manipulate things, or can become merely instrumental to prevent going in many directions.

Imagination and action. My knowledge of the world exists validly only in the moment when I am transforming it. In this moment, in action, the imagination functions, unblocks passivity, refuses an overview. Discontinuities, wave breaks, cell divisions, collapsed structures, boundaries between tissue kinds: where inner workings are unknown, the only reliable participations are imaginative. The complex of state and control variables. The number of configurations depends on the latter: properties typical of cusp catastrophes: sudden jumps, hysteresis, divergence, inaccessibility. Boiling waters phase change where the potential is the same as condensing steam. Random motion of particles in phase space allows a process to find a minimum potential. What is this all about? It's a matter of rage and fear, where the moving grass or built suburbia frontier is a wave prison; where depth perception reverses; caged flight. With ambiguous vases it's as if part of the brain is unable to reach a firm conclusion and passes alternatives along for a decision on other grounds. The goblet-and-face contour moves as it forms in your seeing.

A bibliography has been added as a resource in the back of the book, and has been kept as simple as possible to emphasise some of the indirect perception involved in making *Brixton Fractals*. This is not intended as an itinerary for suggested further reading, or a listing to give authority to the text. It is to thank those who have taken part in the perception and memory that have made the text, and to keep open the opportunity to hear them. I have cross-referenced the poems with the bibliography, but because the poems in *Brixton Fractals* take part in interference and transformation patterns with each other, separating the Resources into twelve poem-groups appeared to be unrewarding.

The chronology of the poems is generally alphabetically indicated. I wrote 'African Boog' first, and 'Boogie Woogie' was already drafted for the Second Set of *Gravity as a consequence of shape* before publication of the First Set, *Brixton Fractals*. In between times the ordering shuffles a little. The titles derive directly from the itineraries of dances in my *Ideas on the culture dreamed of*.

1.   Brixton Fractals

Banda

Took chances in London traffic
where the culture breaks
tone colours burn from exhaustion
emphasised by wind,
looking ahead for sudden tail lights
a vehicle changes
lanes into your path and birds,
over the rail bridge, seem purple.
A mathematician at the turn of the century
works out invariant notions in a garden
every so often climbs a bike,
makes a figure eight around
rose beds to help concentration,
then returns to the blackboard.
The schemers dreamed a finite language
where innocence became post experiential
believing the measurable, ultra-violet from a lamp,
isolated sunlight curvature
made false language what can be done
to separate
from perception.
In a dream apparently without volition
a car burning and
watch myself there
sealed-in beneath a smog dome
uncertain what to try for next.

Midnight: a solo of the Nightingale. Great silence.
Open a gate
against hinged pressure of rust,
white pigment to denote reflected light.
Singularity burgled up the drainpipe,
a busy rush pursued tenderness at its slats
padlocked into pastoral quicksilver.
"If one of my students should one day rear children

in a better way
Surround myself in music, that is physically
forget the dream as a move towards preventing
objectification of vision.
Legal power, completion, smothering,
on the shelf flashpowder and a can.
Practice to assist improvisation
holds onto the pattern of railings
a super-structure of sound-curve symmetry
recognised, and examined, by autodidacts.
A bunch of type in my palm
populates fixed compartments.

Exasperation from a lack of clarity
sighs towards singular objectives
trapped into them
without realising
the peripheral fleets
glanced at knowingly
as an indefinite refusal
of euphony,
or until the variety gets coded
into an analytic container
dropped from a winch onto the quay
When the road shifted
one part lowered
then pushed out a halting arm
over the ridge
carrying a reflex camera
to record the wonderful.
A recollection of a hill so far from London
I burnt lying
in a dream for thirty minutes
and woke in a grove of oranges
smelling of eucalyptus.

[4]

The up and down different to anyone
gravity
or opposes anthropologists of science.
It took six minutes for the exercise
and the lot was cordoned off,
Water Lane
to Brixton Oval,
our future in the air
over the walkway busted polystyrene
scattered,
a sonata for piano and jetplane,
cooperatively struct,
now a mount of cars piled behind a subsiding dyke.

4 a.m. the Hedge Sparrow, shriek of the Hoopoe,
the Song Thrush on trumpet,
a large ball rolls by
hits the sentry box
and the road opens.
On one side a ley line buckles
into the wall of 'The George',
in the machine a solenoid blows
a rush of green vans and police weapons
send the needles into peak
and damage the Dolby.
Your freckles expand and you blush,
a black clock and two batteries,
my fingers tingle to let the blood back
we roll over
temporal inversions or points of view
burn the air,
and memory, slatted into alternations,
begins to rely on the instrument panel
as well as the force
felt in the chest

as speaker loudness increases.
The explanation of the universe gets
considered as shared awareness and truth
a bucket with a hole in it slops suds over
the top of a tiled floor
until we switch it off.

Two electricity lines,
three gas mains,
carry enough energy across the walkway
for two sets of loudspeakers
face each other across the
dancing
visitors at an island of science
see the primitives at work
describe the utility of pilot lights.
The furniture in the room appears to be stationary.
I am half sick of shadows
under pressure of personal feelings
a poet crushes a carton marked 'Shredded Wheat'
in a corn field,
calls it a poem.
Laid out on the lawn
exhausted
the burden of personality lost
in untimed contemplation
independent of unified law
uses signs for other
than what they signify
by filling navel with powder
and exhaling a cough.
I suppose it is in me and coming out.
The quantum leap
between some lines

so wide
it hurts.

The shelf falls from the balcony
shatters,
erupted aluminium silicon
scratches airliner windows.
Two water mains, three petrol pipelines,
a large sewer
in the walkway,
where a tree has broken paving,
build a fire
and get the kettle started.
"The fact is,
when ole bill came along,
we brassed him up."
You know, all I wanted was to recover
without retrenching.
The pipes don't appear to be busted
Just keep it open
I'll go down and see if it comes through.
Telephone wires, and a mile of new road
cross purchased fields
Listen to the echo
of wings' fizz
before we get to them
and resistance
in the reduction to utility
and functions.
Fraught, but underneath it
resistance without armour
as if that were possible,
following a wire stretched across the page
until pen drops off the right edge,

and face
the red background
in the morning
noting where it came forward
in front of a glass bottle
to restate the four-colour problem
broke it there by facing it
The yellow and black road bar
lifts to an angle congruent
to the prison roof.
Bird carpets in the hay
wood. Noon:
great silence
haywire.

Began to decide how to perceive
Dreamed once of where we were going
too precise about direction
said, That's the way to the city, but
I wouldn't start from here, if
I were you
knowing what could be meant in the clang shack
bolted upright
just before the bell came
steel wheels on steel rails
run through the lounge.
It's the city alright
felt in the tropai of directions
the joy and worry in a traveller's back
back from market with vegetables
incapable of doing harm
Leaning the bar into a distribution curve
at the chicken jerk chally
across from the betting shop
or as if based on notions of we have

been here before
or another says that makes such a perfect match
you could use 'em as bookends.
Carried the system down Coldharbour
on the right shoulder
two circular speakers
plate the inner ear just
passing through
your living space
moving with a deliberation
seldom found in poetry.
It happens quickly not as you might expect
takes a long time moving towards
its suddenness and when it does quicken
it surprises. Even so, as I say it,
it has gone and a more deliberate
or expected mode takes form,
changing the minimally real at once into
a memory
chequered in a rebound
cage labelled 'Development'
and unattended box of timed light
marked 'Don't Touch' or 'Volume Control'
as a measure of decay patterns
the Bellman recedes down the walkway
catches my eye
with a Brasso glint
carries a refrigerator on his back
shouting "Ayeyay"
until someone, I think it was Edna,
calls with a camera, "Hey boy, here !"
Gradually I predict the possible physically
and the probabilities that this
will occur. I stand in the walkway
with tracts on good and bad

tearing them
at once excited by the energy
of doing so and recall
the situation
brings the distance involved alive.

Silence: Brutal punctuation of morning:
a Warbler explodes for the last time
an intuitive doubt
passes through the window
regarding the rest mass of photons
at once discarded
at zero.
Enthusiasm sighs
and fear forms in each lachrymal valley.
Blake leans back from his window
down onto the page
eyes partially blind from flowing
writes vigorously across the faces
drawn there, saying
the tear is an intellectual thing,
crossing it out
knowing the trial pended
and anger disrupts thought
momentarily
in a cloud shift, his wrath
blazes reciprocally
stands at his door looking out
into a bright day break
the sirens have stopped
in the near distance a blue spark
leaves the prison roof
an inescapable sadness, thought of
as reflections onto the window
call it condensation

the glass breaks.
I get a dust pan and brush.
The light lengthens and the
utility of cleaning up
sends a shiver into me
it must be getting winter
I begin to cry quietly inside
the strengthening chill
of alternations
Carvings of flowers on a sword blade
catch the spark
I thought I had imagined
then realised
the sword was polyethylene
and the kid hadn't
taken off the tag
spelling out the price of it all.

There was some dancing
but what's really going down
in this male age praised by noodles
an innocent obsession with turning lecterns
coded in digits.
A firelighter in a screwtop can.
The Fireman calls in for the situation report
concentrated in depth of an advance
The unliquidated resistance remains
blank-screened in the blast.
Yesterday I met a man who wasn't a misogynist
felt a necessity
to move into a new mode of life.
The sun energises autonomous
care with weather
and anamnesis
breaks a trend of cut-off

through history. But what else goes,
It is a lovely morning
light adds shadows
The Fireman's report abends the actual
spins in the sky frame
turn from the strictly utile
for aid duplexed
with how things were once better
over the hill
The freedom to act socially now
measured on a breadboard.
Bike boys come down the walkway
rear their burners
almost together on back wheels
at entrance to a workers' council.
She takes a torch into dark room
and light pencils scratches onto the box
circumvents the mechanical
description.
Swept me off my feet,
A policy of time
in a carpet factory operated by
each person each free
moment the space to stretch.
Scratch marks when the pen ran out of ink
still on the manuscript
something potent resides on its validity
unbroken
tradition but
let's actually find out, you and I,
what that can become
with another
arrangement.
I atomise a liquid into my hand
from my breath

it adheres into an uneven smudge
read as it changes colour
the background moves
through it
selectively imprints a warmth.
Thought it might be self-love
flattered by envy until
she saw a different hand there
crumble soil around a new catalpa
a folded sign posted to it,
what it means to forget what has past.
A range of sprays from the lid
sweetens the casserole
He added another pepper then chopped in some basil
The sign unfurled as my head touched
the pillow
spread my perception to speak.

The Bellman and Fireman meet at 'The Windmill'
exchange notes on salvage.
They are who they are
yet remind me of what has gone.
She bathes in rain water at last clean
for the first time in decades
A sign calls me backwards
'Beware. Society Ruled By Men'
The urge to destroy is not only a creative urge,
in the distance a man sings
accompanied by his own hands and feet it
brings sighs of enjoyment.
An apple stew secretes into it,
smells of cinnamon, cloves and nutmeg.
I rub my cells in them
coaxed by such overwhelms I somersault into a grocers
a flurry of wings cross the enlarger box as it flashes

three balls hit the railing complex
the sounds.
If the rebuilt city is resistant
it opens to those who strengthens it welcomes
the travellers on the ways to themselves
Now where are we . . .
I cut open an apple and its wasp goes
hesitant body line made clearer by holding
the sound of skate boards and rollers
launch from a ramp and the joy
wet zings say it as wasps
fed from our bodies surround in changes of light
a dog in the other distance
It was as if the subject itself lost materiality
Bird carpets copied get copied
Value, meaning, determination repeat.
For fun she snaps a photo of the Bellman's cart,
reality and notions of poetic stress merge
simply doing more than two acts at once I cover
the bottom of a warmed pot with Assam.

Disturbing this silence
two chaffinches on two violins
in a biological lock watch
fixed by light chemistry in the eye.
The call of "Let me out," becomes a jig
along a cordon of police,
values from others, opinions, and
deliberately propelled into distance correction.
I am almost what I wish to live.
Outside in the walkway three kids play on wheels
One expects more respects for prospects
includes a desire to manage
A figure of eight with a müller to
slurry tempera on the glass.

Around the World

This gravitational song meted against displacement
The slow movement of holding you
By the lake, deep amid fir and silver poplar
Dream sleep's energetic function
During meditation each finger rayed in cactus spikes
Blake crossed out sweet desire, wrote iron wire
It was the discovery of human electromagnetism
made a sign, opened curtains, revealed the garden
Mouth perpendicular to mouth energised desire

All the weight and attraction that limits movement
A Mercury mix that replaces theft with eloquence
in the face of visitors' astonishment, experienced veritable bliss
A robust memory in the flares of lost and added synapses
So that the vines burst from my fingers

In the space of shape-time
We move our fingers and simultaneity becomes falsity
Sheltered by wall and hedge
Translucent superimposition several distinctions one
synapse   And the garden becomes geodesic for a moment
An *imitation tomb among the vegetables*

"A mango tree under a dull cloth, stirs its tentacles
A rush of calcium through my nostrils

That the complex is Nature's climate.

Passed out in the dole queue from an overdose of guerrillas
satellite bang. satellite bang. hits the
negation of morning confidence and hope

Took a stopwatch into her mouth and spat
Reduces premiums to the political, to the sentence , ,
"and the simple at a discount

"the imitation stage has been passed
In a blue self-portrait the background continues the face
a gigantic plane tree
Given a part, consistent memory appropriates a whole
Flicks mercury in a meter   rolls off a glove

Dealt out cards, silver-foiled dinners and cans
piece. pease. pierce. sleight of hand
Friendship as virtue   an inventive memory combines
varieties of inconsistent features
Take my hand, the silken tackle
Stored associations of the cellular net
Swell with the touches of flower-soft fingers
Rode shaking from the park on flat tyres.

claim of pastoral confidentiality
The return to copying pre-empted by cultivation
its enormous trunk
The net's avoidance of overload and too much overlap
Take this palm to your mouth and fill it with grapes
A Net of Golden twine   many synapses
Semblance of worth, not substance

spawn of an entire lack of interest, but some surprise
The return to cultivation pre-empted by synthesis

enter, stage right, "the creative centre of civilization"
pieces of granite, broken and numbered, rejoined with cement
Its mighty branching and its equilibrium
Hard-wired to compensate against malnutrition and toxic
waste   The danger of important words
In tears clothed, in a dream sleep's shed, avoid obsession
Humane Eyes over a blasted heath
hand holding a book, first finger inserted to hold position
piled granite on the lawn like an enormous potato

Imagination sown meter again then this place beat
In search of ways to reverse-learn junk city
the gravity of its preponderant boughs
Sighs damp down potentially parasitic memories
Mother and child constitutes a society
reservation or rather reticent in flak of rhetoric
Enterprises based on innocence   a pleasant sufficiency
Creative imprecision to emphasise flux of meaning

A future bright blocked by bricoles.

Strapped own earth underfoot to walk base without trespass
Took for exercise of virtue
O sprinkling the garden, to enliven the green!
Dream's random noise shorts-out unproductive activities
Ran out of faces so stopped action in film
A degree of benign limitation
Flummox then repose your wearied exercise

The gravity occasions gone petered against retrenchment
A hard task in truth I attempt
In my garden   face lift   modifying spine shape
Reverse-learning to modify cortex energetically
Floral dress hung from sculptured timber
Intellectual innocence in a pretence to value
Play area scattered bricks painting garden
Then the perceptions begin to repeat
The garden that should have bloomed once

Doubled oscillation preludes another chaos
Confidence beyond consciousness
And do not forget the shrubs
Dream's selection to enhance retention
public elects pinball physics
In the face of wonder experienced a kind of vertigo
Trapped in a cage then allowed to sing.

"Responsibility for the present state of the world
The terror of feeling that consciousness may be
functional   Where are the sentiments of my heart

Simply kissing, with you on the balcony
Into a world not entirely song
Lifted all the baskets   *Even those without berries*
"the Paneubiotic Synthesis
muscle   neuronal excitability   energy generation

to complete harmony laid biggest lime full length in garden
The constantly actualised, shuddered chagrin
In the garden nothing but evergreens
Ungratified desire reminated each moment
Short silence followed by a thud.

Ballin' the Jack

1.

Compassion fatigue—
three loud whistles in quick succession
following a bright flash
hit head on foot bridge.
The strongest trees may survive
width of the flushing band,
a telephone fitted in the garden
on a poolside desk rubber plants.
A doily folded in his belt:
, bulb spot sixty watts, olive oil, honey,
functionally improved recall after sleep.
A moving bang came through the window
modulates permeability across blood-brain barrier
What is it?
a sucrose intake of less than 12 spoons a day.
Sequacious breed reactor
another Take; melodic sweetness; on the prison roof;
indifferent to any importance of verbs
lunch-room physics applied to international relations.
Rain balls
the deconstruction of hope
a varied pattern of bangs experienced as waves:
erasure.
Continuous finger piano
wires over a plane
body colour over pencil with surface scratches
bale out soon.
Equalisation of accessibility beyond private taboo
topological dependence of plasma membrane.
The propeller larger than this flat
at the hub   delusion; greed; hatred;
painted green.

2.

Painted blue
a couple in the yab-yum position
an umbrella spread with my knees flat.
Tropical independence of miasma frame
a muscular energy available to many:
dice gripped then thrown.
At a drive-in, set in curve of railway, an aircraft.
We had to cross the river on a two wire span.
Chopping waves
a dynamic construction
brightly painted fences.
In a given place, to say precisely what demanded
dances, with straps,
learnt from the physique requires interpersonal relativity
different from the posture of surdity,
strengthens muscles of the heart and rectum.
Sequentious freed enactor
three dessert-spoons of fibre offered as minimum breakfast
"What's that?"
modern relations of permanence cross-out with indefinities.
An orang-utan can throw in chaff snow
punctuates proven records with leaps:
, work light, ironing board, oligotoil, laundry,
adroit fingers in his impact
on the pool table stretching, potting.
Even with the keys to 'phones we cross the wires at nights,
one for your feet, the other for hands
strung through trees without insulation.
In the walkway a wig stand
rolling a bright flash
I could see the head in total darkness
a tiredness from exposure.

3.

Wired-up from explosion
didn't know until flash fired
what I had captured.
In the walkabout a mercantile stance
electric fence protecting track from slides
two tiers of chains.
Evening breezes weird moss, fires our sight.
A petal table stretching from the pot
dried fingers rub the thermostat.
, light work, bored ironing, olitory oil, money,
pumiced grooves and traces of hoping
meringues snowed in icing sugar.
Monolithic relations permutated across life lines.
Question identity and gender
enough salt from sufficient fresh produce
extremes of brevity; a history of joy; on the prism root;
preserved in the smack of reflections.
Indignant to the appearance of birds
built on the bowers of paradise
in the garden in front of a work hut
a mossy lawn with objects grouped by colour.
Standard configurations in coördinate transforms
noble lies
Ah, Wilderness! self-improvement anxiety,
on site of a torn sapling a twelve-year-old log.
A sharing of joy and sorrow
cleansed in acidic rain
a continued search for terminal Nature
the vegetable enemy of novelty.
Wung in poverty
an idea of feeling and perceiving the day
in grey ink, Beneath the white thorn lovely May.

4.

Parallelograms overlap his back's muscles
reopen a discussion of limits and vanishing ratios.
She crossed burnt grass to the windmill
over scaffolding and beneath it
read graffiti on play wall where
two kids work sand on dead lichen.
Everywhere homeless everywhere home
heads of watermelon and wood carved from same plant.
Travel literature; works of sex; life on mars;
a dreamer led out of confinement into servitude
works out relativistic perceptions, faints.
With a wad of bark she paints bower with fruit and charcoal
reorients work hut into a constant direction
expels a spitting intruder and repaints green with liverwort
jammed in the kiss of remembering
wears badge of lost innocence.
Activates presence by continual renewal
Questions each movement, each renewal.
In a Brixton queue stopped for lack of identification
harangues slowed through a tannoy
Hands worn hard with broom handling,
scrub pavement, paint railings, polish steps,
dread fingers dub in laundromat.
A lily pond stagnant from dead bacteria,
even freezes, bone welts, frost mires, her plight
two tears of rain.
Fenced in, a society without engagement
now the walkway a gang with clubs
sirens rising falling.
O my Lover and my Friend,
a future blight brocade.

African Twist

"I was an innocent sort of child   1.
    a pluralistic perception of time
    marked by experienced space
just drives me wild
    a small cornfield beyond the garden fence
    low palm trees a huge expanse of bush
    here and there the shape of a baobab
            four broken bricks staggered into two
              rows for a game
turned to look at the sign over the door, simply to remember
            conversations with Gris
a background pulled over the plane of the foreground
reorganising as other
here again
    by the light of a petroleum lantern
    wondering if the crop will be any good
"What's wrong with our life? We go fishing and to our garden
        agents retire to consulting firms to
    specialize in political risk

fast forward on pink noise

    events require you, results inform you,
    spatial lies interpolate frisket.
"the sign over the gate: 2.
    Do what you want
        the desire to organise one's hatred
        with the greatest possible tactical intelligence
Gibbons' carving of Eden under Blake's font
    here and there the tall shape

[24]

a huge expanse
beyond the garden
      a steel tubular frame flat about
            a tree, it must have been thrown right
      over the top
a radical lack of value, a deliberate push and pull
as if free
      asked if there was a calendar, shrugged
      we have a fete whenever we feel good
"We get food and cook it. If you need money you take vegetables
      to market
                   our design meets the challenge
          of political violence and investment
            uncertainties

colour-held ripe contact
pierces snow

      power sign competes the phallism
of polite violation in test meant
      circularities.

"But innocence is hard to beat"   3.
      a new sort of kindness
the local recorded by movements of the feet

      a dozen low palm trees
      here and there the tall baobab
      the same spectacle repeats in four directions
          four broken bricks in a straight line across
            the walkway
avoids subjugation of feelings into marketed desire

it must have been be-bop
it must have seen re-bop
de-pop de-bop
    in the forecourt
    watching a woman trance-dance to drums
"We can't use nuclear equipment. What's wrong please?
                When we ring the bell for help
        we get it These are people not readily
                visible to the outside

light-carried fit touch
in apple

      every time the hellebore smelt
    we get it breeze or reek buttercup red lily
      rhizome toke or size.

"walked towards the exit in cold rain through mud"   4.
      Pound's drama of loneliness
          replaced by exuberance alone
feeling your head thud the shelf
Blake sat
on Kennington Common beneath poplars
over the Effra-Washway

      cornfield beyond the garden fence
      repeats on four sides
      except for a dirt road to the hospital and village
              a twelve inch square frame from a
                  drain left in the empty space
a history of tenderness
an altered pace

going back for a tamtam fiesta
for curing a madman neighbour
"What's wrong with our life today?

You try to get seasoned, mature
judgements We pay well, we pay fast, that
keeps them loyal and vigilant

by chance effected
line-break
meeting pupil

you tie up reason, procure
fudge, many say we stay fast scat
keepsakes, boil and vegetate

"saw the frame of a bicycle with wheels, lacking tires,   5.
on a nail beside it"
beyond parody of the self, a restored strength
the whole body reels then retires and rests until fit
smelling bananas once a stall by Brixton Station
or from aroma know that the twigs on sale could be toked
a huge expanse
here and there a baobab
from the north east corner a dirt road

instead of the frame a cube four feet across
made from bricks in the play area
anticipation of loneliness avoided in production
without domination
a deliberate avoidance of nation in an address

Shat under a poplar tree
watched the moon turn
red
  the weaker
  left to starve
"We go to our garden and get food
      We just recommend good old american
     ingenuity – crawl on your belly
pass stinking weeds across the bananas saying
  they make me itch

the unexpected resulted as inside rest introduced through the eye

full health small percentage straight away improvements turning point
           permanent in London
   adjust reckoned send wooden merry-go
 engine for you to install on your telly.

"gone cold as I enter the narrow door which   6.
  leads up by a winding stairway"
   Mao said relinquish space to gain multiplicity of time
you get old yet learn there is more without
need to project into the airway
  a small cornfield
  huge expanse
  a baobab a road
    a clear walkway and a pair of boots
      that don't match

over the top a destructuration ruled by the alienate
every so often you make a catch
        a bottle of gin down the practitioner's gullet

weighed by materials I feel inner emptiness
insecure from learning he turns to proportions

she releases the shutter, again shifts illusion
the legislature's nullification of the people's referendum

went to market specifically   buy twigs for size
        to mix with chalk carried from Togo,
Brixton stall-girl go-go say

        Don't forget to root it
        and get it good and sticky,
        'fore you put your white stuff in
                        I have a pretty high visibility,
                    so I don't travel   Helping friends is not
                        immoral
moved once,
someone on the box acting unselfishly,
through television snow

unawaited issue proportional space reposed made-known as a consequence of suffusion

imagine a witty rye viscosity
sold to unravel sticking
commends this time quarrel.

Read Klopstock, wrote and counted
until Lambeth turned from the stars
wiping arse on the sun

accretion

Eyes lift
from a book feel the condition
complex body
temperature and objects
adhere to
the read
singularity
in a region of spacetime
cosmic censorship
others call coherence neither light nor
anything else escapes
living's troposed alternatives
a stone ejects
from a pond.

Atkins Stomp

1.

"I don't know how humanity stands it
I think I'm in danger of losing altitude
In a catacomb, hope for future bliss
My hand writes on a tangent to cup spills.
At bottom a low trellis, beyond it a narrow lawn
Climbs a stool to feed meter for gas
"The enormous tragedy of the dream
No capacity to express demands for tomorrow.
Next door she say she wants to scrub my potatoes
Escape over the gate with a peach
On poster a dove sips neon
Disease promoted as health. London.

A cat walks garden wall to the railing
the path still goes from the gate
Sent in the 'district support unit'
Trees and shrubs with dead foliage in summer.
"Take that smile off your face
Two pound of maggots wouldn't reach tench,
        that kind of rigid
Laced on the koran a flowering meadow
Repast glows in the heads.
Ate all I famished
"three young men at the door
, digged a ditch round me
A tree in the centre, then a low wall.
Bounce a ball against a brick hammering pavement
Decides between gas and hot air
We exhume the past, dissolve parliament
"I don't know how humanity stands it
Walked down the table to where the chairman sat
Organising rain with a sponge push

Bone heads in rows
Shits on daffodils showers them with sod.

2.

How they purchase will depend on their choice of food
Huge profits from 'Landspeed'
Started with anecdote lead on conservative angst
Destruction of flora in a circle unexplained.
Splintered beauty
A kid hops the walkway,
says two elves can beat a wolf, and repeats it
Behind the front, a row of trees and flowers.

"having run into the future on a bicycle
Beat of two forks pulsed out of phase
They decided therapy should involve poetics
Helicopter over paradise.

Explanation jotted on a menu
the moon in her tender green meadows
Wooden heads   heads of watermelon
Turtled by ribald-rid offenders.
Lifted menu   popped it into her bag
Dicing down Mayall Road
Research into primeval echoed polyphony
"I been told the process ain't nacheral.

An opaque greenery shifts vision
Different colours arrayed in a bar
Thought that hinges on definition
Pollute fumes from rose ash glow.
Sad to feel the ribs of his cow
Dead honeysuckle twined round the railing

Housing seen to diminish rapidly
Encircled by a ribbon of officers.
The air was made open
Helicopters over paradise
Are you kidding?
Essential repeat mauves in the head.

3.

The alleged ubiquity of confusion
Rain no longer of the process
An oil-soaked naiad rages through blood
A runner play stream grouse project.
Pulse of two beams beaten out of phase
Distinguishes smoke from fire
Those are voices singing is an illusion
A dense hedge made only for looking.

Tackled the chairman on the lending leap
Says two elves can beat a wolf and repeats
Listen to the baste of the reggae
The stars differing colours
come into the park they say is dead
Amid hopes drown our hearsay with one keg
From my feet you can name me as a traveller
Cross town to be with you, Let's fuck
I have a understanding of selling and buying food
Escape over the gate from a tiger
Opens the air to its vacation thuds of apples
Stimulation animates through absorption box.

Reorganises into war and pride
Remains cube a sponge from a carpet
Spent in the disturbance resort bullet
The wall has not been opened.
From an inability to communicate
A siren
Increasing speed into a cul-de-sac
A cascade instabled from a sponge.
More geese than swans
From an inability to communicate to
another locked within
Population inversion amplifies in beat.

4.

The allay of ubiquity
Two pounds of anchor wouldn't reach bottom,
        that kind of tide
Massaged my igloo says breathe into pain
Unable to say the simplest.
Spits on window sills flowers them from pods
Pushed back a few feet, replaced by a vegetable wall
The actual colours and shapes of unspoiled
Without resort to says words can be born.
In the space of the picture the boots
Explored by means of touch
From bed to the levee, tarragon scent over omelettes
A runaway greenhouse effect.
Touch, a complex including eyes and ears
Distil bananas in a dustbin
Sent in the disco retort spoon it
Stimulates emission across spontaneous drive.
What's more she say she plants blood for tomatoes
Boiled boots for dinner with ballet shoes

high seas move over curvature towards carpet
Asymptotic touch a massage with a sponge.
Coherences limit of spatial depth
Rimes with foot to feed the metre for gas
The strange wilfulness that describes essentiality
Doppler waste in person ample pies in heat.
up to the gate, and from the fence we can see outside
I sink in anger a refuses attitude
, something about being singular i think
Studies shoes to understand where he has been.
The alleged ubiquity of pi
Dissing bricks now insanity's standardised
"It's a DITCH all right.

African Boog

Went dicing on my bike
Disappearance
Meaning given by timbre
Relational invariants from a flux
She lives in advance of her days
Speed
Rooks carry aubergines over Tulse Hill station
He hung an 18 foot blackboard in the garden
In all the beautiful continuity of hope
The innocent
She crossed Hillside Road with her sun lamp
Thought confused by recall
A car in flames
IN the climate
Distress of need
Moments when the go different two-beat series
These are birds is an illusion
Confront
Down the escalator that ascends
Constituents of multiplicity unaffected by transformation
Pauses, and, introspections
Their own terror
From his mouth produced a net curtain the length of his body
"Surrendered myself to magic, that is physics."
Watching myself burning from a distance
Spectacle it unleashes
Authority, perfection, oppression
Moments when series go different the two-beat
Improvises from consistent memory
Violent in itself
Her attitude's beyond music called indirection
Configurational relativity, the sound of language
Dissing on my skate board
Population
Your patience is exhausted with someone

"To catch a fly on the moon"
The default of the garden's charm
Each other
Hooks vary auburn jeans overt until fashion
Discontinuous strata, unsteady sediments
Closes behind her the gate of childishness
Always ends up
All the oranges, but one, turned blue
Tripped up by details
Down Electric Avenue in a garbage press
In future war
Overlapping fourths with thirds
Essential and accidental property.
The sound of the heard and the played
With dirty hands
How to count the stars while riding a bike
Moments when go different the two-beat series
There are birds singing
Deterrence
Cycling into seeds and mud
Relativity on the flip of invariance.
Autonomous order disorder
Truly violent
Juxtapose time a-cross-rhythm
Your forehead blur-laps beneath mustard field
Two moments when the two-beat series coincide
Only the turn
A metal box in flames
Constructed proof for consistency
In perpetual *leans* accelerates
Against the military
Fools about contemporary with falling
Topological correspondences unfold similar linguistics
together.
Extemporise from inventive memory

Superversive
The *shapes* of the figures 2 and 3 make music
Loved to dance
She enters the enchanted garden
Because insoluble
At the velocity of milk in a vacuum flask
The rough edges, the false starts.
Just pumping up my tyres
The spectacular
In opening amazement a tulip stretched beyond return
A misdirected intensity of discovery itself
That this isn't universal experience
Simulation
She's lost in a mode with a fun loop
Stratigraphical completeness sifted in differences
Expectations may be high
And appear suddenly
Foam, issued-out produce, a certain learning commodity
Spans far longer than experience
Just warming the pot
Terrorists, public opinion
A direct hit on the waste basket
Undecidable
In a purple lean-to, accumulates
System which
Walking down the drain and laughing
Contextual and stylistic alteration
Buckled beneath a fruit stall crying
The stupidity
Counterpoint reduced to fracture two and three beats
"Tables, chairs, and beer mugs"
Spontaneity from electro-chemical decision
To exterminate joy
Juxtapose pitch notes melody
Disappears in bluebells   wood-light   may.

Moments when the two-beat series go different
    Actuality can be the meant
Absorb myself by watching
"He looked *so innocent*"
Crouched in a doorway mumbling
    To palm all that is reported
Juxtapose harmony-notes vertically chords
Every turn within change;   joy and worry
Just ratatouille on the gas
    Innocence
Brixton market frequent, Brixton market full music
At odds with results from everyday
Just imagining pleasure
    MAKES all the variables
Tempered by the moon on his shoulders
Instead of feedback through the eye as a basis.
Perhaps an uncommon or personal experience
    A minimally real event
Orangutans guessed, but one yearned it was true
    Few study deposits for as long as a decade
    Its shades slow with promise
        Flashing
The chair left through the window
    The proposition without deduction from other propositions
    Play drum with the drums being heard
        In a maximal echo chamber
    Two moments when series coincide the two-beat
    "The laws of nature's independence from the choice of
        mollusc."
    Tigers are in cages, tigers are in cages
        The contradiction in situ
    The mud of perfection
    Relations that have a finite ideal
    Just come in
        Does utopia

With joy and fear small thoughts at large
The process being followed conceptual and executive
    together
Skyline in the window
    Patterns how many years
A civilisation based on dancing
Assumptions on visual evidence reduced to syntax
A mix of two-beat moments invigorates texture
    To open for measuring time
Flames
This volume determined by the size of needle
Just smiling as you
    The personal alters consciousness
Shape of your eyes dilations condense brights
The particulars of each plant heightened by common
    structures.
Absorbing the memories chemically
    Changes
Two moments two-beat series coincide when the
Stars detail variability shows an average everywhere the same
Horizon into the window, the siren
    Initiates
Older parallels and pseudo-parallels overlap
"Tomorrow we went to the forest"
Just playing in the mud
    To think about a problem publicly
Shone from a helicopter onto a tulip
The rug rolled away
More often than not represented
    Political to value slowness
At viscosity of spilt ink vacant tasks
    Stratas record positive deposits, but what else happened?
Blowing metal into tumblers of cells
    Had taken the possible
JUST ICE

Immediacy at the thresholds structures activity, that is
    perceptions
From the balcony over the tulips, the church
    The society made by men
Juxtapose timbre vibrato to patterns vertically and
    horizontally
Opens a glow-out red jacket in a crowd.
Asleep in a hammock, accelerates
    Dance collaged into reel
Conversation and your breath bell
"It happened that I found myself tomorrow"
Four playing cards on a box in a crowd
    Implosive order abolishes
A language based on tone and timbre
"No one will drive us out of this paradise"
Seduction turns to exploitation
    System of repression
Her stare reft thought in a winder
    Span's illusion independent of the probable.
    Stolen wallets on a bread crate in a crowd
        The order of transgression
    Indiginer and invader overlap
    "It was tomorrow"
    Space toys on a pavement in a crowd
        The old bacteria of law and cultured intrusion
    Speech patterned horizontally and vertically
    "Ya! Ya! Ya!"
    Or enchantment becomes repression
        Value, meaning, determination
Asbestos beauty snapped in a rain storm
    Reality a requirement for perfection
    The sound of memory-played with memory-being-absorbed
        Excess of rarity
    Two moments series coincide when the two-beat
    Without limits, the universe of these beings is finite.

A street in havoc, exasperates authority
    Law, point of view, evidence
Lifts from a spring board into cloud
"Temporal separation a tenacious illusion"
Every turn of the path seductions
    Entrenching the desires of others
As best as you can rapped from the brain bourne
    Jump on bike, figure of eight around rose beds, to the
    blackboard.

Bel Air

1.

At last it octobers, a tremendous
mist descends on my head
trip a cat
an obo hits my incisor
I fall back
"Good Morning, this is the News"
Is this naiveté or integrity—
this simpleness or confidence to gaze
with intelligent vitality with
numerosity a
splendid buzz from a razor that,
spaced out on a slowed down recording,
reveals a fluff in the magnetic arrangement.
This is Europe
It's not even a terminal.
Forget arrangement. Stop.
Replace with manipulation. Stop.
"Thankyou, but this gets us nowhere"
A Burglar near the end of the century
looks out over his balcony
and reinterprets the State,
Everything now appears to take place outside
Work's quantum determines the permanence of violent conditions.
Of course he's sick of it!

Shall we follow?
He leaves under the sign
'Café du Dôme'
immediately we are living in a Still-life
The Painter steps through a gate of bamboo wicker
a radar pulse at centimetre wavelengths
strikes her left cheek is
partially absorbed

no one attends to its flows relations
adjust in due ratio
The room is in the rest frame
manifested by drops on the glass
This is the situation. What happens next
requires our happiness.
Each blink tampers with record of it.

2.

Shielded by these particles autumn
offers astonishment.
Instead of organised hatred she
involved in disorderly performance
made necessary by the floods
weaponed through the fence
an entourage of western medicine and humiliation.
She paints at the gate
the struggle of objects for supremacy
The Burglar crosses a room and knocks on
my eyes, He touches my mouth
with the edge of his trembling,
He frames me with my own perception
as it internalises.
A yellow glow seeps past the doors
he leaves open
The community buy dogs
to protect him.
Boys argue furiously over
their video systems
The Burglar sells his watch.
The Hamming code suggests
a drop-dead halt.
They are calls for a clean-looking page.

The Painter moves from the gate
persuaded to contain impatience
through unexpected calm and firmness.
Lamentation and grief become the patterned
stable world, make guests of those
who belonged.
She matches the found pattern
of a star map
into a knitted pullover without
a look forward to the outcome except
a knowing of its warmth
recognised through texture
It lifted the debate of production
and autonomy out of the Burglar's
bag still wrapped
in newsprint
and opened it out.

3.

The children recognise the cloud shapes a
mathematician codes as corank one.
They see the dynamics
without knowing the internal parameters
and one girl trailing the drop-offs from
a running toy
turns to her now stationary vehicle,
"We better go inside before it rains."
The Burglar leans out of someone's window,
lowers a box of sand
onto the walkway. He
is insecured by men and scraps of paper
permitting him to live.
The Painter follows a path to a simple hut.

In the wet an umbrella loses its
commodity function. She
rejects this. Professionalism's
insistence incites her anger.
I am tired of the news
and play through a contemporary
Quartet at twice its intended speed,
swapping one note for another
then dropping loud breaks of sound
mid-rhythm into my weakness
leave my initial appetency
for another weave.
The reflected radar pulse
returns through the window with a
second. The star map begins to craze.

There is talk suddenly of mortice locks,
with another, hasp and staple,
inside an alarm sounds
from a car in the road
we know, beforehand, we are in a city
We call this knowledge but
are also in out of place
no room to move without limits
The Burglar rings a bell for help
It is a mistake
We are alarmed and our
vibration changes colour
randomly our rhythm chocks
and my breath catches hers.
She leaves a half ounce of casein
to soak along side the alcohol
and ammonium carbonate
It is enough to fix the image
made of the Burglar

She continues to walk away from us
up the path to the hut
without identity, carrying
a torn drawing marked 'Studies
for the engraving: Adam and Eve'.

4.

A reader follows the marks up the path
occasionally losing balance from
may be
synaesthesia
stopped short by the figure
of Blake, kicking away sand and pebbles,
joining the path
naked beneath his raincoat,
locks my eyes.
I imagine he has just been
writing a tract on astrology
"Irrational action," the Painter notes,
"From rational self-preservation."
I respond to the stimuli realised
as alien to my experience.
The mathematician adds a calculation
through spurious adaptation to realistic needs
This paternal acre is a colony a
usurped matrilocality
"The stars," Blake could have added, "Advise,"
mitigating fear of the inexorability
of social processes you create
as reader.
The Burglar moves that
everything negative
is due to the outside

A flight of birds,
released to tell the time,
superimposes heat patterns on the star map.

This creates a spatial illusion
One colour appears above the other
through its transparency.
What may have been noise
gets read as fresh knowledge.
It carries understanding that the
collective distribution of virtual utterances
creates the social set-up the
institutions breeding
value judgements about innate tendencies
or irreversible actions.
The Burglar moves over another barrier
behind the window
unaware a camera
records this onto film.

5.

It becomes apparent from the film
a dance is underway
The Painter moves towards the open
hut. The path has muddied
before her from heavy boots
and the overlapping tracks
of a bicycle. It creates an
apprehension which increases her
exaltation gives it momentum.
She stops on a stone to sustain
deep breaths and
reels from them.

The smell of elm bark accentuates
this. Women like her participate
in the war against coöption.
What she creates prevents subjugation
by the State, but it is no longer possible
to point out exactly
how.
Yelping dogs remain quite distinct
from bird life. Yet some of
the sand she threw at her painting
remained there, became gems there,
what blew back from the throw
took some of the slurry from the path.
She enters the hut to find she is
there with three others. They sit in silence
smiling.
A loud bang moves through them,
followed by a draught.
They all rise and walk down a
second path. She begins to
question this. Her palms are itching.
A playback is underway on a wall
with accentuated wood grain.
The silhouettes of the viewers
interfere with this, but
clearly there is no figure on the
display. They watch a window open
and net curtains lift. They see drops
of rain move across the floor. A
chair lifts from the corner and
moves through the window. There is
a sound of shovelling. Everyone
begins to get the creeps. Their laughter
ceases. A box of sand shuffles
across the floor to the window.

"Stop it!"
The Painter turns to the others,
they are asleep and lean over themselves.
The smell and colours moving in the
room complex. This pink noise
becomes an image
set before her.
"Stop it!"
She turns to the others but is now asleep.
The Burglar switches off the playback
and moves to the window.
It is raining. Its breeze
turns a wooden toy on the play box.

"What's going on?" the Painter asks.
Their coldness astonishes her.
In such a set-up of standardisation and
threatening sameness, she is positively
cathected. Their silence becomes
the voice of an estranged society.
The pattern of the star map at her feet
has settled into a streamlined adjustment.
What it now tells her is useless.
In the walkway a man carries pavings on a
trolley to the sanded mud and begins
to lay them down.
I lay back on a pillow to feel his
movements recorded by the light on the ceiling
and the sound of his ram.
The loose bricks, old frame, and some
discarded footwear, form a heap in the walkway.
"Its over the top," the Painter said,
"It alienates the reader."
There is an emptiness
measured in proportions.

Democracy is given a high rating
on the opinion poll. She takes down
a bottle marked 'Pure Water'
from the shelf,
"Shall we fuck first?"

6.

"Anyone else want to ring the bell?"
the conductor asks.
I cross the city road to the walkway.
On the slab a scraped block of ox-gall
to break the tension
The Painter is in the garden
following a thrush.
Children are roller skating with
a ball on new paving.
I lift a tract from the shelf
and weigh it. No physical
entity escapes this surveillance.
It frees all concern about issues
of internal consciousness—violent
motions, unknown forces, tortuously
curved, even multiply-connected
geometry. Dealing with a point
simply makes contradiction. This
swarming, the mathematician
calls multiplicity. "Its a
matter of intensities," the Painter adds,
"And velocities and temperatures and
decomposable distances,
"You have to use your
intelligent body
to *feel* it." So much needs to be done
to know the consequence of shape.

Boogaloo

1.

Citizens break into loudspeaker
space fills
with a yellow
glow from the walkway
bricks
lift are thrown
repeatedly
a discussion ensues
interruption in the room
a buzz
saw takes out a dozen trees
in a row
breaks a power line.

There a shopping list
written across the table
conversation here
relates a burnt-out bulb
to an empty honey jar
inside an oil bottle
last traces
refract the glow from fluorescence
green hues
vary intensity
in tune
with a silicon index.
Fingers produce wave forms enlarge
our space
from Martenots graded air
moves through ear cells
improves our appetite
I dip into a bag
for glue balls

take out a Mars bar.
We measure
moving colours.
They are almost free,
parametered by spins
in the bag
experiment
we measure their leaps
in terms of weight:
predominance and and emphasis
The yellow changes
temperature and mood
reduces
distance
makes a cell
of the living space.

2.

The auditorium starts to turn and
the lifted orchestra
starts to turn inside
intense pressure
on my chest and forehead.
Gradually, the audience
lift from their seats are flung
against moving walls.
Held
against concrete, my clothing
taut across me
we spin with the auditorium held to the walls by its turn.
Simultaneously with this violence,
electro-magnetic field volumes
the whizz in our heads

increases and the floor
opens
an indistinct memory.
Over this the orchestra,
a clustered ovoid, appears to
hang
like a gas, it isn't dusk,
streamered
spectrum then flashes. The orchestra ball
begins to shrink into the cornet
funnel shape of the chasm.
A shrill of echoing distinctions
speed up
I want to hold on, yet
to speak
catch
my companion's eye
A door bangs.

Someone came in, as if
in anger, slammed
a mortar board,
in an open hand
yellow rock
Hold on!
The auditorium stopped we
started to fall.

Sat across the table
from each other
He made some of it,
we said, Blacked
out when the floor went.

3.

The milkman delivers ½ lb tea
through the letterbox,
a label
    QUALITY
       BY
    CONTROL
removed from the bag
has fixed onto
a loudspeaker.
Pressure appears to increase
Natterjack choruses fill room
Hold on!

It is dusk,
its impression
creates a relief
They go to a concert
music by Varèse and Ravel,
there is laughter and sleep
interrupted by catarrh.
Blake notes, It remains to be Certified
whether the Fools hand
or the Physiognomic Strength and Power
is to give Place to Imbecility.

An Inspector
climbs from a bike
to check a cast cover
in the road makes a rubbing.
His meditation
recovers a sense
of boundary she has
between ideas and form's

autonomy and conversation
recurs
when I lose my temper
I cry
or brake
just before
to avoid
a car ignoring
a yield.

In morning
his stomach rumbled
an invention followed on
truth and resemblance.
Held out his palm for coal.
Massage
reveals
overlapping parallelograms
from wood-grained concrete.
The geological function
of my nervous
too obscure to discuss
for long
yet avoid speaking of strata
They came out of the air
lock
glue balls spattering
our bodies
poppin', or somehow we were dancing
from the vibration in our birds.
The direction clear
if firm
        "Never rub out,"
The Painter's tendency to probe the most vulnerable
never cruel

a gaily spotted snake zigzags page, says
Adam and Eve and Pinch-Me
went to bathe,
With full brush made mark
without question
washed out remaining paint.
Simply the presence of a hundred crocus petals
lifts our Velcro.

4.

Walking the path
together
inside
it could be dawn
the sound choruses
their silence
vulnerable
as pledge of safety
or falling back
on the chair of preconceived ideas
a misunderstanding
of the figure
creates hazard they
sustain in readiness
to receive in
the making
a difficulty to achieve
meditation
itself creative.
His sharpness in her breath
disturbs him
on the subway
beneath a sewer

live kids discuss
potential of
batteries with her
without analogy
to the State's
dismissal of community use.
What my roles are

continues
to break notions
of who I am
derived
from finite mathematics.
Presses to hold
onto the speed.
Screen the loudspeaker wires
and around rings
form a jellyfish
on a wall sheet
engraved movements of television aerial
spinning around room.
A skip lifts
onto a lorry
jumps over the sound of interruption.

Prepare etch, Trace figure language,
with
Buy honey and oil, Make drawings
derived from direct perception of
sewage repair, after
recall of infernal method Blake
cracked head
on protection door of etching cabinet
made light
crack

focus on
rim of the jar
burst the
memorised glow.

acuity

Agreement to assess
what is in
    focus ensues
a singularity
    narrowed in spacetime
the difficult of
    a fixity
unsure image
    corresponds to reality
massaged by coincident
    alternatives to
understanding
    perception
    shifts

Boogie Stomp

It's easy being alone, but who cherishes it. cooperative motion.
accommodation of transient energy. fluctuations. not an intrinsic
cycle. happiness without local strain on interchain bonds. for
instance, the exchange stability of beta-sheet protons reflecting
structural flexibility. combined interaction between particles.
turn out more than you'd get by using the parts. sum-up an
overview. then reject it. put down the phone. again. continue
diagram of a crystal. condensation on window. cold identified. ice
caps, glaciers already melted, retreated. sculptured land. viscous,
just underneath it, adjusts, to decreased load. the dimmest flash.
a postglacial rebound.

Perhaps eye strain. an average of seven equalising particulates. a
simple proton. tectonic acts. relaxation of impacted areas.
rheological and viscous properties. irritation, but no real
discomfort. circadian what? male periodicities. not agreement
with the world, yet happiness. the sun spots. a solar core rotating
about twice observed rotation. thermodynamics of becoming.
recognise this whilst the feeling hurt. core flash mix without
prediction. stellar change. lattices of breath. puckered hexagonal
rings of water.

Stacks in sequence. ABAB. or turbulent plasmas in a pressure-
drop. a magical study. ice as "one of the strongest materials
known". ordered sets of oxygen ions. compare stars of different
masses enveloped by tenuous plasma. chromospheres, coronas,
with ice subjected to high dynamic stresses. fractures by cleavage.
creeping solids stress-directed. diffusional flow car. slow carriage.
taking each breath. as if that simple. blood volume in the head
above minimum. facilitate recall. letting it happen in the same
environment as that in which learning occurred. position as
multiple quantity. drawn in as forces on the diagram. draw a
vector label it **v**, times the unit vector **i**. frictional losses recorded.
dot.

dot. eight cans. each once held tomatoes. each identified, labelled. space between a can inside another. Toscanini, told by his bassoonist of a break on the lowest key note, paused in phase space, "It's alright—that note does not occur in tonight's concert". name the grass. cost of the seed. method for cutting. cost of shears. servicing mower. volume of water. sharpening shears. frequency of cutting. plants weeded out. where's the seed from. where's the mower made. where's all that water from. what's the soil underneath.

Exercise. forget the counting. bone cracks. another press-up. count. short breath count. enough of counting. vision as memory plus perception: possibly. a creep law calculated with a power law dependence. dependence on what else. stress marketing. cross the room and forget. activation energy equal to energy for proton rearrangement. adjusts. an adjusts. from experimental lout. science policing. intensive analysis on every moment, each transition. temporal dimension extended to the whole process. incalculable motion. in the far, for instance, decline in spectral sensitivity. perhaps bruising from over blinking. unaffected by absorption in the lens. unaffected by self-screening. affected by distress in another.

Order in ice two, disorder in ice one. glide of dislocations. rhomboided. melancholia. periodic scream. optical light modulation from red dwarfs. understanding as an extreme. manifestation of star spots. the use of niacin, or simply yeast tablets. look into ice six. a structure of two identical and independent frames. chains of tetrahedrally linked water. mutual interpenetration of molecules. self-clathration. (one of the components enclosed in cavities of the crystals of another component.) difficulty with the principle. difficulty with least action for continuity. eloquent error. typed as whurr. overstrain or, reposition the table lamp. eidetic analysis of perhaps. a language and an energy to speak. but you're not here. until the 'phone, or bus across town.

Two different environments the same time. alone in each. how to mutually recall. avoid tenacious illusion. meet you at the sands if we get out of here alive. periodicity of intense love and inertia. dealt with in the physicality of this expectancy. a such (where shape offers spatial affinity). not search as renewal. not legalised or rational. the independence of pigments prior meeting without notions of mixing, or analogies of new colour. rather, configurations of tactile boundaries. almost definity. instead, the slightly possible.

Many directions (misunderstood as spread). each hormonal event sets a readiness for the next. another ovulation. or pregnancy intervenes. watched as ice six formed at room temperature. compressed water in a gasket between sapphire anvils. ABAB. computing the photometric parallax. assumption of alternativicity. crystal another comfort. seat of disorder over stability. stability repressed alarm. dark noise. scaled to fit the zero peak in the flash. generalised laughter parodied as six crystal systems. glide in the structure seen on dense planes. dislocates glide after a steam bath on the glide set. bonds cut. dissociates low energy stacking fault.

Science vocabulary in hysteresis. measured wheezes. dislocations moving on the shuffle bus. going for reorientations. an intellect steeped in empiric lockjaw. ice compressed into silicon or whatever it's forced to. begins move. cuts through obstacles to analytical solutions of thermodynamic lattice problems. imports techniques from particle fields. makes Ising lattice problem arbitrary. the good chthoned into strata. hierolatries. increases of nearest-neighbour interactions. a tensor algebra to derive a focussing. the elegant mambo.

Changes in size shape orientation. you're not here, that's difficult. too easy to be difficult. the approach involves bringing another dimension of analysis, to relativise the contents of this analysis. oscillations of bioplasma. affined to a change in male responses at the same time as the partner. the whiff of your attention. in the presence of the magnetofield. whiteness hums in my head. on the 'phone. suddenly a tapping in the phase space. why we need to know about control. pre-empt its ability. eidetics and empirics moved to a phenomenology of vision. a search for alternatives to coherence. range of perceptive angles. parity not conserved. radio interference. eye strain. telephoned conversation. a focus on sound that changes the phase space as well.

Black Bottom

Laned on my bike
black High Road
iced from repetition.
Apocalypse
came down the hill spitting
Never saw him
Simply fragments
Frozen refuse, A
dry throated discourse,
A metal gas
to stifle analysis.
She smashed milkbottle
as bus moved sat
and cried
on a back seat, her head
contracted by a rear-view glass
on the window. At the entrance
hung over
a raincoat, a walking cane.
Energised desire shapes Her
gravity.
The colour introduced on an apple,
already forced
into ripeness, forms a series
of translucent flakes on a dish.
William Blake makes a tracery of a figure
binds it to his headache.
Leaves follow footsteps. through snow
perhaps a traveller
runs away from noise something tearing
his ankle. A trembling
image rises out of darkness: Blake holds
his head between fingers
dry from acid
Bright Work diffuses

through forms of thrilled consciousness
becomes apprehensive only to another.
Gradually the workforce of
a marginal elite
burn down hill
to read latticed recurrences
in the ice.
"Oh, constructores, Oh, formadores!"
At the junction with Streatham Place
a telephone Engineer
sinks into the road onto
a green path,
a moleskin folded in his belt.
On line voices sing
unseen
a Photographer
moves her feet across a wire over the road
lowers a sun lamp into the pit.
It bursts with yellow startles
he pauses, then pumps
water onto the surface
from a tributary of the water-shed
moving towards Kennington Common.

On the traffic ice
two skaters superimpose
figures of eight emulate
moves through
the pinching of two singularities they
push through a yellow box:
the ice cracks as the lights change
It is dawn and tulips.
The Engineer watches the path
of lightning hit a distant terminal
switch. Break

open a pack of Luaka Bop tea
leave pot to brew under a spiked glove.
I bike up the flooded High Road
The Engineer lifts bundles from it
to decode the district. It leaves a sponge
The pits area lines the holes he
leaves endless: its
volume has vanished. For a moment: silence.

That is
what the blackboard says.
I rest on a kerb contemplate
ice shards my tyre jaggd with
glass.
Each fragment changes the vocabulary.
The sponge that gave the image of a black cube,
without hint of its increasingly evanescent structure
being constructed inside it,
gets cut with a torch blade
synchronised to precision by a satellite
transmitter to prevent its curve.
The Engineer calls the sections
carpets and kneels on one.
Immediately she is reminded of the
Ewbank Stomp,
What's on the blackboard? she calls
A large articulated haul
drags a propeller between the Photographer and Painter,
Push and Pull, the Painter says,
What?
The creation of depth.
You mean colour? Love enhances colour.
The Photographer grounded,
sent the wire trembling a trace of lower 'E',

[68]

I've busted the prism.
Brixton prison?

The noise of the workforce
forms a Moebius strip in front of us
a discordant cry needles
the ice. They're nourished
on reflections.
Stop it!
Boing.
Stop it!
I held breath
They watch clouds
move over the road flood.
The Engineer pours tea.
Distance from him increases
with synapse counts.
The upper limit
of reciprocal interactions
breaks. There is a smell of hot fish.
Local densities ensue,
patterns between them
cannot be discerned.
Truth is derived mathematically
in a quiver intersect
of independent lies.
Restriction enzymes in an orangutan
correspond to those of the Engineer
They form a single clade.
The Photographer improvises
beyond mustard-seed be-bop,
an angry
dismissal of everything that
came before.

Her condition is diagnosed as *leans*
Record of her energy playback
is censored
marked 'Unprofitable'
derived from a loss of orientation.
Her periodic pain moves out of cycle
A light-carried issue in a reposed,
proportional space
pierces snow. The Painter calls this Song.
She crosses the High Road
singing, so sure of her lover's beauty
she is incapable of resentment.
These rational delights
bring her to carefully tidy the disorder
before the government search her apartment.

The Engineer rakes sand over
oil burns on the path
to the windmill. He spreads dust on snow
and readjusts his watch.
A man in a raincoat
taps his stick down the path
recites Góngora.
His ears are burning.
He sees the Photographer's arms around an elm trunk.
One hand can be discerned: it trembles.
Between her hands he images an equator
her body a sphere of energy
perhaps equal to the elm's it
bounds without meeting
until knotted in a six-dimensional space.
Blake closes his door
for a long time turns a key
in a delicate lock
and listens.

Six-space?
A Mathematician, a Poet and
the Engineer sit across a map table
on the High Road
to begin analysis of the ice.
The Mathematician opens an English copy of
Klopstock, 1811.
A running walk can be checked from
ground prints
alternative hind-foot-hind-foot footfall sequence
reads as one foot close to the surface to take
body weight should the support foot slide.
Every so often saliva has frozen, formed discs on the path.
Six-space is a delusion, the Poet says, It's
noise, reminated each moment.
Information, the Engineer notes, transmitted over long
periods of time, deteriorates.
The noise can be heat, or radiation, right?
It can be mutagenic chemical. The molecular
clock runs faster than the genetic, It relies
on noise for the controlled introduction of novelty.
You mean balance of conserving and radical change?
What's that mean? the Poet seems irritated.
There are problems of measurement and scale.
And imagination, the Poet adds.
Are we talking, asks the Engineer leaning back on his chair,
About resilience, persistence, or resistance?
Perturbations need to be stated spatially, the Mathematician
turns to the Poet, Your richness, connectance, and
interaction makes instability. My evidence suggests
that local stability can be observed.
But you won't wake up to the complexity of observation as
participation.
I'm not concerned, the Mathematician says, With
the successive destruction of individuals. Entire generations

will be grovelling on the Earth. All volition assembles
to form schemes for destruction. We are here to examine
the ice, the cracks, and the shape of this great cloud
of opinion points.
Energy and time cannot be simultaneously measured, you know that.
From the cloud we can integrate over one variable
to get the probability of the other.
I am on an equal footing with what I see, the Poet says.
No, the Engineer interrupts.
The Poet turns to the Engineer, Your system
is acceptance of death.
The Mathematician laughs, he rides a horse into the
green path glowing with a golden cane in his left, a
storm bursting from his right, towards a riot of flowers
that enamel his Paradise.
The melons are flat, ready for serving, buttercups
have straight stems, raspberries
spring into baskets between their bushes.
The Mathematicians breath visibly leaves his nostrils
freezes on the tabletop.
Without deliberate perception, what he sees
repeats and trembles.
I stride out onto his plane, feel vertigo,
until I induce a horizontal depth.
I can shatter this ice, this encased sublimnity:
I can prevent your sleep's expiation and encourage
curbs to your euphoria.
The Mathematician ignores this, walks over to the ice
to contemplate its structure
as if its crystals focussed his energy for thought
The Engineer walks across his contemplation
to triturate this illusion. The Mathematician watches
through his windscreen, then laughs.

I question, the Poet calls, the temporality of narrative,
and use its maps to make their records obsolete.
The Engineer lifts a bundle and carries it to the table,
A thousand confident threads, he says, Hold friends
and not one of them would break that.
That's an illusion of the future, the Poet argues.
The Photographer interrupts, We reject
stoicism as vanity. All that impedes lucidity
and hampers confidence crenellates the present.
It's a roll of film, the Engineer jokes, spilling
his tea. His cup leaves a white circle. The Mathematician
starts to draw a tangent to it. The Photographer doodles
a shopping list on the tangent line,
writes, HYPNOSIS,
across the Mathematician's copy of *The Interpretation*
of Dreams. I picked up one of the Klopstock volumes
Blake had marked. I was crying
and wouldn't say whether it was joy
or a sorrow of amazement
In pleasing confusion,
We're breaking we other's bones.
The Mathematician and Engineer contested
strength in an arm wrestle across,
what the Engineer called, the concentration table.
A storm hung over the High Road as I wheeled
my bike up the walkway for repair.

The Photographer strung a row of peas across the table
aligned them with a meter alternating their poles.
Halfway along the row
an electric shock snapped her arm
The Engineer startled in disbelief

Boogie Break

1.

Took the walkover at the park to change transport
in a squeezed State.
The noise first expressed as random in phase
fluctuated and obscured gravity. It
shifted the discourse into a gap where
measurement relied on quantum non-demolition.
The Mathematician took notes on a microchip blackboard,
obscured from a saxophone Busker by a bend
in the wall. Out of a desire to minimise uncertainty,
enhanced by the squeeze,
a massive irruption of bright colour
in soft, contrasted hues
gave a volume, tore the Busker from the wall
and suspended her,
cut her image surfaces into prism clashed edges into
the non-trivial significance of her libidinal investment.
Her energy glowed.
In this phase-sensitive, nonlinear interaction
the Mathematician was provided with heightened
signal-to-noise rations. It presented the discourse
with data bus technology to reach an escalator
with many user sites, but no repeaters.
As the Mathematician noted,
No classical analogue exists
for this State without ideologemes.

Such technical language exhaust-fumed
reflection, left my pinched head in
a juxtaposition of buzzes and roars.
I biked back to the High Road to witness
where they reread the ice.

2.

The Mathematician leaned over the ice
measured the displacement of markers
to compute its creep,
as a function of stress, the ice's and his.
He assessed the space between ice and road
a structural mediation between knowledge of its route
and an inability to take it. He looked across to the Busker.
Areas for articulation of what was here and there
and the grammar of his accounting
were in breaches of noise echoes.

The limits of this analysis relied on recurrences.
Periodicity in lattices determined his seeing, allowed
arrangements to discern production and segmentation in
how he described it. He determined how
such might be organised and thus controlled
through the inscriptions of his shape in gravity.
This resulted in the construction of a simple anachronic model,
a paradigmatic reading of a mythic discourse
which correlated coupled contradictions.

The experience was frustration-dependent on
the idea of finite repetition in infinite lattices
to articulate invested content
independent of its manifestation
in the didactic discourse Freud
or interminable anthropological diffusions
had offered him: between
the uproar of shared experience and
the rebellious processes of ideology and value systems
manifested as if in a static mode,
as a base for dynamic generation of his narrative syntax.

His first calculation excited him, it followed
thermodynamic properties with their expected phase transitions.
It relied on representation of a lattice and sexual well-being,
to allow a suitable choice.
The apprehension of myth at its every moment was ready to
develop into narrative reflected in the foul sky's
prefigurations on the ice surface. A storm
or his departure could not change this.
He discerned phases between nematic and smectic parallelisms
in an attempt to avoid description of the surface ice
as skin and his galvanic response.
His narrative utterances he made independent of investment,
and took its constitutive elements as isotopes
in an attempt to avoid what his unknowing would invent.
He began to focus on temperature and material concentration
to interpret the saying as a desire to realise his programs
in the form of description.
These were enunciations of virtual programs, a syntactic
practice consisting in the transformation
of his virtuality into actuality.

This was difficult to understand
through the couples of mass and heat flows.
It meant the introduction into the surface of his perception
of a wanting, a perception that included a guessed at seeing,
a wanting that prevalorised the solution converted
into a description, then into attributive utterances.
It became the actualisation of wanting
irritated by notions of consumption.

3.

Thus through reflection and analysis
the Mathematician distinguished values
as a formal criterion for understanding
narrative structure. Nevertheless,
the wet and the solid were in a fractal dimension and
required a dialectical procedure of domination and attribution.
It burnt his eyes and gave him an erection.
In embarrassment he relaxed back at the map table
and began to show hysteresis as a problem
of percolation between free movement and the lattice,
where transformations of the virtual to the actual
became substituted as domination and the desire to dominate.
Performance thus showed itself as
the characteristic unit of narrative syntax.
A naïveté between what is thought and said,
and what not thought yet expressed.
It's as if he believed these conditions form
themselves, irrespective of social life.

The freezing point hysteresis,
where the ice neither melts nor freezes perceptibly,
was within this gap for prolonged periods the Poet
guessed at as being sufficient for dream sleep.
The orientation determined by the road and the Busker
corresponded to the relation of sequences of implication
at the space of manifestation,
where the road's ground provided rules, so to speak, for
ellipsis; and its surface, rules for catalysis.
Fragment manifestation, carried by implications,
proceeded towards reconstruction of the narrative
in a reestablishment of integrity.

4.

He therefore started again, this time to specify
what might be discussed from what he perceived directly.
He searched for algae
trapped in ice-water columns.
He looked for pale ochre
as a sign of brash or pancake ice.
He found frazil ice to indicate ice growth.
It was a search for the interface
where congelation ice would form as an established sheet
and thicken the floes, where
dreams are ghostly shapes discernible only through
the gravity of waking.
He began his string of performance orientations
from two practices he had discovered earlier.
He derived the trajectory from the initial wanting
through his knowledge of how to achieve it. From his
ability to achieve he knew he could do it.
It became a control over the ice presence
as an extension of his powers of production over its surface.

The Engineer interrupted now, to indicate
that through the use of a sapphire-anvil
squeezing could be simulated and the deformation
could be profitably studied.
It was as if the narrative was at once a discussion of
an investment in euphoria and impatience,
which would lead him to suggest that the cloud,
the Mathematician looked through to create his analysis,
had in fact been an aid to prevent the destructive
notions of infinity.
The kind Blake, through his analysis of conditions,
continually subjected himself to.

The two of them continued their search
for nonlinear creep, or basal sliding, until the light dusked.
It seemed the relentless destruction of any remnants of
their capacity for fear and hope.
The topological syntax of transfers
organised their narration as a value-making process, and
provided meaning.
It was the process of expectation derived from
fantasy of the social and
led through a sleep named Daydream
which continuously exchanged with its hegemony
into a representation of what the want wishes to do.
It put their action back into the traditional male role,
a bleak circus in opposition to life, as it was discovered,
into the invention of sublimation.

Birdland

1.

An image of the Engineer's model
shudders in a basement
as sand stabilisers are loaded.
The left arm bright gold, the ears glow green.
Out of its head energy spatialises
overlappings of spirallic fields.
A figure appears to attempt flight,
it may have wings, yet held to the floor
accelerates towards an openness through liberation
of its partner, unseen from the pit entrance.
Is it male? What is there to say
concerning child birth?
Its presence takes place
between table and pasture, at this moment
takes space between road and underground river:
it is named jouissance:
The arrival.
It brings experience of radical separation of self,
like child birth, produces an object of love.

2.

In the morning television I carry
a cylinder of heat in my embrace
down a garden path labelled by the placing of stones,
Hey Bellman, someone shouts,
puts a match to a felled lime
lengthways in the walkway
with meanderings of drama
thought I was moving forward
lost ground
in mistakes, with grinding gaps in what I know about
fidelities or reproduction. By chance, it seemed,

back to the path I had opened
Its trace visible in footmarks and
potential infinity to an unknown fold.
On certain days, this morning is an example,
I remove my helmet cross the path
with a slight intoxication
to check the lime has been properly extinguished.

Endless destruction
makes Brixton
Call it the coexistence of prohibitions and
their transgression
Call it carnival and spell out jouissance and horror,
a nexus of life and description, the child's
game and dream plus discourse and spectacle.
On the edge
of death High Road, the Busker
starts up a reel, it begins as dance interlaced
with anger. I guess at the ridiculous partners
that perform. The Busker dances with
her saxophone
'Ideas of Good and Evil' are subsumed into this nexus,
production knots and
unknots paranoia
Blake stands his ground
on the Common asks, Are
        Her knees and elbows only
                glewed together.

3.

A woman came down the walkway
lost in transport
exploded her language at a kid

with a stick
restrained by another who breaks
the rod across his leg,
We've had enough, got it! We've had enough!
One hour later someone has dragged
a felled lime onto the walkway
Its leaves make a green path
A pack of dogs surround this, yelp
out of phase. Down the High Road
a new siren on a police weapon
fills the walkway
It leaves a burnt fizz overhead
grooves the mud plane on the roof.
Next door fits an extension to his aerial
changes tone of CB interference
in loudspeakers makes audible
amplified pulses from a geranium
in a Faraday cage. A poster snaps the letterbox,
Come to Paradise in Brixton's Coldharbour.

4.

Beneath helicopters
Brixton abandoned
challenges the closure of meaning
so far removed, nothing will have taken place but the place,
flattened housing for ecological reasons,
fuses with a beyond, a successive clashes in
formations, memories of bodily contact, but
warmth and nourishment do not underlie the air.
The Mathematician
gets on the subway in a pinstriped
with a microchip blackboard. A spotted handkerchief
matches his tie. On the back of his head someone

[82]

has singed a domino it
matches his ear rings. As he starts to leave
his accounts, he pulls the arms from his jacket,
sets them alight.
The effect is laughter,
an imprint of an archaic moment, a threshold of
spatiality as well as sublimation.
Suddenly a path clears Sleep relates the squeezed
State to a lack of community He leans
towards me, Last night, he insists,
I had a strange dream.

5.

The imaginary takes over from laughter,
it is a joy without words, a riant spaciousness
become temporal.
The demonstrative points to an enunciation,
it is a complex shifter straddling the fold of
naming it, and the autonomy of the subject.
Wearing four tones of grey soap I
read photocopied pages on lighting effects,
the Mathematician battery-shaves and makes
notes on squeezed light using a notation
echoed by remnants of beard clung to hydrogen
on his trousers. Subjection to meaning gets
replaced with morphology. I become a mere
phenomenal actualisation moved through a burning gap.
The irrational State insists on control.

2. Breadboard

Boogie Woogie

1.

She came down road in a sponge hat
Dazed but walking, I remember
looking back
Jewel-hit eyes in a snow storm
On a swing in a garden
by the windmill
On the Cleaner's face
timed light   administration
Felt only as she recoils
Innocent?
I draw back from a kind Stranger
She crosses a pond then one-legs
on a rock
Lefthand commence to rub
arthritis
I *feel* my Hollowness repaint
the seen.

Talc reinflates distraught
breath box. Hey!
That swing's for kids!
Long experience watches, chooses
epicycloidal profiles
She inspects a torn button
The train out of the city
literarily prolongs shape of the city
waves of lichens on burnt-out wastage
Willowherb analgesics and
nettle curatives for wheezing lungs.

2.

A child smothered in toys
skids a ski slope
from the city.
I think
I was in the wreckage
I think one of the survivors
got me out.
I go to the swings when I'm angry
A cold hollow spot, an aching
I could not *give up*
Used ice for a ramp
they flew into the garden
The oscillation of balance, contraction
and sprung expansion not obviously
in rhythm
You simply take
speed and flavour enhancers
with you.
She takes my breath

3.

All I could see hurt my eyes
Lowered egg into water
turned the timer
It was as if she
was in pursuit
without letting hold of the Stranger's hand
her watch across
pulse skin movement
zig-zagged into winding
tension and elimination
of balance knocked banking

One system presses jewels for pivots
into spring-supported bushes to absorb shocks.
Worked 8 to 5 fitting condensers
into salaried circuits
Routes from the city ARE the city
Take in the smoke and
stare out the lights, This
wreckage moves

4.

with extreme regularity
run urgency
self-winds
dreams
with external sounds, perhaps a watch
or rust-hinged gate
regarded by market as Off-track
naïveté, radicative
depths.
I think I was in the city, or,
heard two bells sound a
recovery of debris and satellites
Sometimes a vast stretch of
quiet, like a lake,
interrupted by jump-jets.
A tendency to pattern connectedness
away from external appearance
Broomed stock
market floor
recorded tobacco coffee and steel
Rest
as an intimation of a future
tracks the radioactivity which resulted.

Asleep on the swing night into morning
watched that perpetual feeling
Coleridge imaged
an animant self-conscious pendulum
continuing in its arc of motion by the forever
anticipation of it.

5.

Scrub marks across geometric floor
record details of industrial health
In the lawyer's office
the Cleaner looked to
the Stranger's wrist glow
Ideas on the culture dreamed of
dispelled.
Lit another dog-end, moved
tide scum over white ground
laid brush into suds
turned them grey. It adumbrates
the slow noise
the swing's squeaks
almost exactly interrupt.

Bop

1.

To see it simply isn't easy
She came down road in a sponge hat
calls in a focus then another.
I pull Brixton
one by one
I pull bricks down
I am the Cleaner
and my hat takes in the weather
just as my brushes impact an interface
between hands and
the lawyer's office, stock
exchange, the railway carriage.
I look back at
who I am feel
the emptiness.
The sponge is not infinite
but its limits are immeasurable
You can't see the atoms if someone's
speaking, I mean if I'd zero angular momentum
I'd be spherical.
Lying on tea-room floor a
ball of energy, feet
up and blood
filled head.
Violence begins with each of us
to end it.

2.

Even when we are not in love
he is grateful for being loved
without spoilers to drop the drag
left two-storey windowless concrete

on external vehicular ramp.
The surgeon conducts
intimate searches down the barrel
of a double bogey seven
If we thought his stretched hand was to greet,
we now see it serving to fend
off male fantasy
Of course we were also
right the first time.
His watch finished and smoothed on his elbow
underestimated radioactive waste
The hot components on his tongue
pepper the back of
his mouth until
whole milk sours the
heat out
of anger.

In such a basket of currencies
three people beg outside
Brixton tube
call up Amnesia
on the Read-out

3.

There a scurry
a flight of stairs
then a landing
A flock of dogs
hit pavement
from the terraces
Jebb Avenue garden
lament on radio

salt onto
ice, maybe
accumulator like
Two people
on the wall
breaking bricks
from underneath
themselves until
Bell sounds
closure.

4.

My end is in succession
houses fall
are destroyed
considerations
at 50
on the by-pass
walk passed out
onto pond
edge soft
weeds underfoot create
apprehension and delight
No flamingos simply hay
rolled into bales out
of white flowers tree tops
against bright grey cloud
superimposing onto clear sky
moving over the windows buried
in my innocence's abyss
Radium mines, Papuan heads
some milk of childhood
Rebuilding this community

could be another century
Soaked to the skin in mud
coat lost crawling the first
lot of wire then three rabbits
in front of nose the traffic
seems endless
why am I doing this?

    5.

This morning like a daisy
Fast aircraft loud bangs a kid whistling
Stood in shower of yellow rocks
loaves of rain
Fourteen million watts ten times a second
I watch you write this
from a metal cabinet
steep roofs bright light
basket cases with hoses
in all those greenhouses
severity of sentence predicted on
a revenge index

a support building joined
at the upper level with
two positively vented air locks
change clothes in the popping
decontaminate
link to main computer
a meal of bells bulleted
all both Morning & Night is now
a dark cavern
14 tons of glass gather
fossil light.

coda to Boogie Woogie and Bop for Albert Ayler

Laid on his back
ache
a sudden leaves fall
many still
green
record their mitogenetic radiation
describe them
perfume
we roll on
throw our arms around
trees autumn
but never know this.
When you're young
it don't seem to matter
if you tear your
playhouse down.

Boston Monkey

To a critic, on the bus
a witness describes his position
just before an explosion
in Jebb Avenue a
molten litterbin on the corner
a large group
powerlunching in Town Hall
"I want to speak

It's classified learning
Trust
misunderstood as other
Planks dropped from scaffold
signify gunfire
A crane lifts
sails from the windmill
Slow boom of a gong
speaks of memory acquired
inside
surrounding wall, a quiet,
dusty garden, a quiet
dust on the magnetics
misunderstood
because that's exactly
what it also is:
another's potential.

A history of locality
"Got my gear down Rye Lane
Hopelessly marooned
recorded trees in link fences
Across Brixton Hill takes
in metal through nose
without modification
inflection

immediate
The wit that brushes Aluminium bronze
on black paper.

It's a digital milk crate
the amount of mere quotation that encumbers
Dressed up like daughter in dance shoes
pulls wire cage
across walkway
Activity on nerves
aids knowledge, says, Makes happiness
"I have nothing to say
to grasp the first hopes held out
Put chatter beads
onto throat box
turned on loops   Draining
its static through bus pole the
bird cage spins and rudders song into screening.

It's classified trust
a history of markets
Rushed finance resulted in a wheeze
following thoughts to their extreme
It's a scratch wall
whack box
The softness out of tension
in a morning's cleaning the scrub plane
Attention to the slightest variation
alternates enjoyment and deprivation
The cells from slant culture
form gametes by starvation
What it is as potential
a splash and a whack box.

Aubrietia came through the cherry blossom
as window shut

Keep your noise down can't you!
Organic substitutes
make a bulb space in soil
It's classified turmoil
a few old trees
without modulation
quiet filled with steel-gauze and shavings
Witnessed photobehaviour in a colour shift
the structure and excitation maxima
"On that stall behind the computers
Bird in Bird cage
Whack box.

The Critic notes
Who owns destination
does the cooking
Keep the noise down!
watches kids
play in dust sheets
Leaves line before it
breaks black edge
Lifts carpet
An organic world-view the
lightening computered State
waste tension processing energies
tinfoiled wind, handblown in storm glass
Witness glitter dust, dose-response curves
540 nanometres.
What it is as potential
wire caged,
estate cordoned-off.

The stop-response
positive phototaxis
Flash Flash

[98]

in a whack box
Lifts carpet
takes out dust through a tube
Intensification and remission
Gravity, cohesion, elastics
Irritability and electrochemistry
a kind of ebb and flow praxis
Perpetual revolt alloy-screened
The Critic on a mouldering stair
in sunlight, flicking
metaphor and metonymy,
rings a bell.

Aubrietia   cherry blossom   explosion
"Let's reject happiness and
periodical consultation
The score indicates many changes
on the squeeze-box
with all its adequate stops
A threshold negative phototaxis response
just before the wangs
shattered window perception
superstrings came through his forehead
Trust misunderstood
as potential
Life as duty, ascent and conquest
State educational severities
appear disappear on a wave front.

On Tannoy
the Witness
reads through crackles
scratches the Critic photoreceptor
Reruns the inaudible self.

Break-a-leg

1.

Yet somehow a mocking clown
fastens onto any activity that catches the
face a tourist's movie camera
The shows alternate plimsoll and walking boot
In one hand a cane the other a rattle

The aim of the research
to compare the spatial characteristics
of position sensitivity to awareness of movement

Four planets stretch out to the right
of the sun in the morning sky
We landed on the opportunity after Noon
without dependence on time perception or our emotions
Without weight
There were stonewheat thins with Monterey Jack cheese
south of the jet stream

To speak of the moon as an opportunity
unleashes the ghost of its presence
and colonises the speaker
underdevelops civilian economy

I take out my pollution handbook
to hear the news and start counting
The rate of beats decrease
as we descend
into a lower temperature and question the biochemical
clock
Calcium carbonate drips onto a peak of stalagmite

In transport with therapeutic seating and minimal
ploughing

without jellybean repeats
the competition melts
The manufacturer's input of Faith *and* Money
creates confidence
burning tumbleweed on the edge of Interstate 25
Says, Unleash the leopard I stand astride,
This is VCR time
Here we crash cars before they are built
for people that don't yet exist

At 9000 feet with 120 air speed
radar and lasers probe our structures
west of Alamogordo
without Go-Star's navigational alternatives
to commercial radio and ground control registers
we locate a kink in a pipeline
Later follow it across the Los Piños
mountains to the drop zone
At 8000 feet the land is remade 3000 feet below
scrub, roads and housing become
lichen, petroglyphs and pictographs of habitation
Geological lines crossed by animal tracks
Paths of nomads following geology until
break natural formations,
leach alkali, hang ristras, then move and leave
Animal Sun and Water signs pecked into desert varnish
alternate rods of snail mucous and graffiti
"Gean I can't get no feed,
I can't wait for you, April 1st 1930"

We need preparation time
the proper frame of mind
to ensure effectiveness
A photographic alignment of the land and its image
creates synchronicity

Lifting in a cabbage crate or simply walking
at 7000 feet
hæmatite and
lizards spiked on barbed wire
As time passed the clock descended the winder-rod
and shadows lengthened
Men of iron with syrup ropes moved downslope
towards
rock alligators and blue bushes
soapweed pinyon juniper and sagebush alternate
coded
speech in a glottal cough
In shock control I listen through ear sponges
on the gas-phone to an inversion tube on the horizon
"We're at point 14 diverting traffic there;
We haven't got anywhere to put anymore at the moment;
Is your cordon in?
All buses are to be stacked;
Over."

A generation of controlled crashes and fly swats
puts an X on the end of the runway
Digital clock time
Clasts of sandstone and sideritic ironstone
form surface alluvium
Mass wasting in a downslope gravity
partly conceals coal interfingering marine rock
a periodic transgression and regression of the sea
and filth winds.
We circle the house
and the occupants waken and feed us
But don't touch fingers on meeting
On the ground in Real time a pinyon drips a stain onto
tarmac   It is the only moisture for fifteen miles
Snow geese form another horizon in the binoculars

A Yagi boosts the end-fire receiver and
a voice repeats, "The Range is hot," from the missile site
The place becomes a cinema
The effect of tourist speed on landscape
An aesthetics of disappearance
a dromoscopy in which we no longer reflect
Black lava fixes its flow before white sands
In a hologram of a human skull 2 million years old
a leopard's canines have penetrated the cranium
dragged its kill out of reach of hyenas
This excites the rattle trap of mythology
preserved in paint by a Blockhead
transformed in film for analysis
the plague of intelligence

The research notes cabbage patch dolls;
a spinning cow on loco-weed; and
greasewood burning on the range

Sinking into a cavern more than 700 feet
takes 3 thousand years
Clothing goes yellow in floods
of damp and moth iced visitors
I look out into successive perspectives
The sun sets and rises in a single window at once
Pink sand, yellow cake, broomweed and meadow larks
contrast reading the instrument panel
at 4 inches of mercury suction
We hit turbulence
Any divertissement loses grasp
Subliminal comfort multiplies quickens consciousness
a vivacious reflection
to guard off a conditioned crack.

2.

With the need to lock into personality I
hit a button on the whack box to
start the dirt talking, Here
it comes now
start the talking, Here it
comes to nothing in the essence
trap, Comes to
needing
abandon
Take me, Says,
Clean the limescale on the structure
and take me to
my seed, Say,
Let's get rooty in the
wet house
electric burn in the wet
house,

From a Deptford balcony
an aerial ascends
at 70 degrees,
Below it a fishing-net.
The only occupied
flat in the block,
three shot guns in the
lounge; derelict buildings
all over London.

A vertical system transforms horizontally
where identity is ambiguous by a two-choice
smiz. Plural identities form
a variety of vociferations informed
by transformed systematics and

the Clown steps out
starts eating from the trash-can.

The Re-Destruction of the vertical stripe
and horizontal band, the Re-Dissolution of line
and edge, the Re-Obliteration of texture, the
Re-Abrogation of asymmetry, the Re-Demolition
of shape . . .

Arm locked on a glue bag to the railings
wards off blossoming in Water Lane
Leather belted to the extremity of a thunder clap
to mitigate the fatigue from wandering
under the spread
It broke out like a rash after the experiment
a whole gallery of sculptured heavens and hells
covered up to strengthen the monument.

Behind windows nailed boards
glass smashed and the boards signed
with love from Joe.

You are invited to squid on the worm gas
trapped within your own subjectivity
Vertical spears horizontally fixed
These harmonies of violence
an observer finds aligned to self-control
They let the cat out
to spray the illuminated
rattle traps
the lumber of an awkward estate.

Breaks

1

It is only themselves that they love intensely
We should think things had been turned upside-down
In 1981 he took the television aerial
Spun it around the room
The Clown is ageless.

In the absence of a fixed masculinity
a jellyfish formed on the screen
Its position made ambiguous by movement.

The process of recovery gives the impression of absence
The self consists in my thought
I became that image in 1985 at 7000 feet
spinning in a light plane
Without weight
until continuous postural adjustments
and matches against surroundings

The definition of the other being a disease
nerves burnt the orientation
Unsure of gravity's alignment and
relationships to position.

From experience of satisfaction
buried out of sight in the depths of their rest
the vertical and horizontal
were assessed by reading
an instrument panel under the screen
as the gauges notated lean.

Searched for the correct distance
outside the aircraft.
On his jacket
below the spine,

painted in gothic script,
the word 'Discharge'

The represented figures turned
Side by side, their likeness makes laughter
and rotating the painting allowed
facture of the somersaulted ceiling.

Distress and pain of bodily sensations
as the Clown started laughing.
Ghetto-blaster
Police siren
Helicopter
connected directly to your system of
drain control
Learning to skate in the summer
at 8000 feet
scrubbing the roads and housing numb
from itching petrol and picking habits.
As we went to press the condition
was said to be stable and comfortable
       Tests are being carried out on the
            ultimate effects of the bullet
            which entered her left shoulder
            and grazed her spine
       What we do have is a new type
      of inquiry under the new authority.

Hypochondria of the erotic
the basis of all this wretchedness
catches camera
face rattle.
A rotographic line of the landing
traces the culture ramp
Rifting in a rage crater or limping

at 7000 feet up
the blood blizzards
spiked on charred fire.

The Clown both observes and participates
catches a blur of planets
in a moving sky plane
and blushes from agitation or
the smell of vegetation
peached in a lozenge.

The importance of the purpose
This arrogant force which checks and dominates
handed weightlessness as an apparition of presence

At precisely the point that should have been under
investigation
a slick of yellow fog
Impossible to tell whether position
was established on the basis of how she feels
or how she fits
her surroundings

To indicate the disavowal of lack
to stop living inside himself
he puts a daze into the
dial glass.
The vertical intrusion into the horizontal
combined into the overall queasiness
and the smaller breaths
The tension thus is between
stratification and breakage
between the island of the tonal
and growth.
Next to the Hall of Machines I suggest

they put a Hall of Accidents
train derailments
pollution
collapsing buildings
That's what I say in
The Aesthetics of Disappearance
The main idea is the social
and political role of stopping.

There are biological considerations in its favour
against jellybean repeats
It's as if the animal became domestic,
raged its fill out of preach hysterias
This ignites the battle sop of apology
served in pain by a Blockhead
formed infill for paralysis
the lag of television.

The correct distance is the opposite of the feminine
a hardening of the heart
remelts the lava
north of the missile site

A charging of the ego
as the radar light starts flicking
and drop out over a basin
into successive perspectives
We have breakfast and dinner at once
in a chorus of red and yellow
fast breeding the inset annals
at pinches of cursory reduction
We hit turbulence
Any diversity fuses gasps
Subdivides fortunes into the cash nexus
an invidious flexing
two yards off touchdown.

2.

Asunder in a giddy state
prattle raps
with stray elimination
leach the fat out
and sever binds of ligaments to sell role
frees barmies of violins
through a gridded fence
trapped within bones of subjugation
raw in vital switched on the worn gag.

Whether above or below
gas rashed the bored sigh
grinds wind hailed balls

Ruddered up to tension the movement
a roguery of skeletoned cupboards
I rake out the trash after the impediment
asunder in bed
to mistake the factural squandering
feather-felted to the tremor off an under-trap
fools glossering with faulter canes
Harm clocked on a screw rag to their failing

Bending the bucket, the centre lost
alignment and the text became obsolete
without definition of taxation
or graphic meridians

Starts heating from the cash pan
the Clown steps out
by transport cistern attics and
aviaries of vocal rations in formal
wizz. Puerile densities form

where density is figured by a two-voiced
vertical question trans-born or on tally.

All over London
lungs detect billowing's
free short runs in the
flattened lock
the bony ocular
bellow in a frisking vet
A severity diseased
on aired dissent
from a department baloney.

Election birds in the net housed
without
Without need to lock into personality.

brend

Since invitations are for power
he invested in regularity
insisted on established facts
and thus interpretative subjection
The real produced necessity
and glob of uniqueness centred
into the multiplicity of a subjector
his proprioceptive valuation of entopia.

Sure, give me back the fiction
of projections and I'll hand you
the probability of similar scenarios
Recognition, phenomena,
chaos, and subjection hope to
contribute and the invitation
is yours to accept:
RSVP.

Busoni

The thing valued is separated from the valuing of it.
The long suppression of the weak by the strong.
Not to express what is expressed by the action
"Sweeter than honey."
Levitating over two feet from the ground.
Existence deprived of innocence by intention.

Butor. *Passing Time* again

1.

Drowsiness
window-pane covered on the
rainside
litdrops, a myriad
mirrors
restring parcel of
feeble light
drizzled down from the grimy
sealing a thin blanket of noises
enfold me begin to thin

2.

This process of draining and
viscosity
to deliver me from the lethargy
which had
expressed by
the action
gem bright green across the room
from the ioniser
to ward off
pressing entropy

3.

Window panes
covered on the outside
hundreds of raindrops each holding
a minute
reflection of the ceiling light
globes

4.

Staring through
dense, smoky, sooty air
the blurred flickered
on the slack, coarse woven, accretion
screen

5.

The sky
a little darker each time
the lights
kept on a little longer
a film of cloud, uniformly grey
hides a blue
less stretched and aromatic, far
more remote
sensed than sky
that sequence of glassined pictures
a view controlled by gum

6.

The rain darkness thickened outside
my window
the drops, like thousands of
transient, tremulous mirrors,
clung for an instant before running
down

Bristol Stomp

1.

A gazer's belief in estimation
determines a defensive measure
Took train to end of line
to look at horizon
suburbia in certainty
Not weary of this, simply not challenged.
Returned to destination
over arches alongside
     the Blakes' house.
Consider horizon
reflected on the pavement
Mud-weeds
A rise of fog over distant
interrupted by a descending jet
It ceases turbulence and orbits
over browned sulphur
flushes a lake of red oil
into the reflections.

2.

Out of description an
obligation to perjure persistence
Shook strain to bend or lie in
to brook after happiness
despair in comfort.
Notary office, simply nonchalant.
Returned to destitution
overt arm-chairs, a long sigh,
     "Happiness has its rights"
on the main gate. Confrontation
a blaze that breaks horizontal
insistence

cracks a hammerhead
into splinters on a magnet
solipsism's last ditch a gaze
over ground saltpetre
rushes a cake of reed foil
encourages perfections.

3.

On Lambeth Road
saddened walkers hold their children
regain firesides with vague melancholy
that a joy has ended, a happiness completed.
Cling of bramble and nettle to barbed fence
a tenacious illness
where politics places existence
as a living process in question.
This cosmetic behaviour
          rationalised
determines an offensive pleasure
Mistook pain to depend on design
a book about the horror zone.
The targeted buyer confronted with
unsatisfied needs
a huge army of wage-dependants
as a production-collective
reproducing war.

4.

Blood reeds
a rhyzomic fog descants
Charcoal, saltpetre, sulphur bright.
Out of ground elixir

a mirror image of desire
inside walls of black stone
cultivation with equal care of
delusion, greed and hatred
This high status given to
       illusion
the technocracy of sensuality.
An abstraction of use-value:
surface, package, persuasion-image.
The saddened with projectile mentality
An unfulfilled aspect of
the gaze a language
taken
for granted.

Bugaloo

1.

This approaches what she calls the innocent
without being first or banal,
That stuff of desire
he approaches as memory field
vetted by a shower
blinds of sporadic breaks out
a lack of lack
in the traum's long blink
"You stink!"
she's shouting
but this isn't the dream,
"You don't even know what love is."
Below the skid slope
the mail van halts,
"Where's 81?"
Interruptions construct
the city plan
unfurls from desk to floor
Distances clearly marked
powder the print-out
The data tablet
derives from a race
circuit
bent crash bars
expose the profligacy
from tedium.
The Fireman opens his cabinet
makes an itinerary of explosions
a phone number on
the back of his hand
becomes smudged formula
he treads on
the plan crops his footprints

confronts
the Examiner
at nine in the Burnhouse,
"Will you never learn
the changes?"
"Truth and beauty,"
explains the Engineer
are flavours
like up and down or

2.

Those times of innocence are past
He relocks the cabinet
bolts all eight corners
with an extra turn
The traum-valve leaks a
perfidity
They haven't even met
he can hardly call her a friend
sends her a toy
to put on her telly
It's innocent and casual enough
until he says, "She tempted me"
like any politician
he has a private lock-up
I've been tricked into believing
in him
wearing a knowing grin
becomes
flabbergast
where a third watches two people
in love
He gets all the experience he needs

in the still glow of a garden
"I don't want to be bothered with girls either"
sits until prepared for longer flight
the hair-raising silence when alone
with the Alone
a confinement seen as self-absorption
in which he can fly out into the fruit-trees
and be easy there
a general theme of restriction
becomes a deliberate separation
from the din.

3.

The Fireman becomes a back-room boy
like the Critic
hopes to stop the committee
from doing the fatal thing
without actually meeting
on a power lunch
The garden becomes a springboard
From here the Poet could become
somebody, a heeded voice
"The human creature is inherently
puzzled or betrayed" grants
the reader a momentary
loft
I betray this on each twist
of the gratuitous and its
exchange with efficacy
An apparition of hop and youth
leaves the unresistant garden
as it starts to burn
It enters the apartment at nine

in the mask of the Examiner.
The Fireman consents
to there being a potential consistency
and conceals all disquiet
about the primacy of perception

They overlook the foliage
with lively satisfaction
Using holomorphic trade-offs
he toys with the idea
of applications in twistor space
with imponence.

"There's an alternative
"to least action."
The Examiner pulls a cord
of wire across the window
and snaps it onto the glass
They both anticipate
shattering
The only sound is an empty
can moving down the walkway.

The interactive gravitational field
breaks symmetry
She
gesticulates with her thumb
across her foot arch
and plunges her whole arm into
a tray of paint
"Now!"
The Fireman pulls a map across the window
and the Painter
marks it using a handful
of feathers, an arm dripping paint,

and occasionally kicking up
towards the same space
cans of coloured powder
"Now!" she calls
and he returns the map
to flatness
"Praxis," she says,
"follows love".

Buzz Step

The Painter lifts Blake's unposted note,
Do be my Enemy for Friendship's sake . . .
She turns the mangle for an impression
and a roller jams a ridge of blanket
This effort of the present itself
displaces the weight
From the window Blake
crosses field-harrows of inscribed soil
She recalls Hayley's wife:

Hope of freedom,
not a free engaging
her leg chained to the flint
of the summer-house
dominates her future.
Her thrusting anguish
the gravity of the instant.

I wish I could help, surrounded
by this fuzz of green distance, of wing beats,
face in hands, huddled.
The Painter tightened the type after the roller freed
A double employment of mallet and will
In the gilded frame, blotches, flickers
According to the light
I could retreat into the depths of
an aquarium, instead
tremble in the foreground offensive
Rally against tears and comfort   refute calamity.

They recheck the ball of wood together
The mangled text exposes a thread of green
samphired against a roar over Knights Hill

Rockets pass as quickly as through the walkway
A child screams from its cage mimics their power.
Blake mobb'd and robb'd in a bread riot
Devours the arrogance of nothing to fear,
in dried linings.

Alas! wretched, happy, ineffectual labourer of
time's moment   Give me my madness that inscribes
Do not chain my feet to Duty and Reality
Tears the self against consumption killing by degrees,
against indifference to lived-in gore
beyond the garden a cemetery with headstones
carved to commemorate the lives of pets,
A medlar tree and fruit stench, beneath it,
shielded from wrinkling.

Doubled up with it, his freedom
turns responsibility, shows
anger to friends, mirth to the errors of enemies.
Progress from assumptions of high symmetry
and equilibrium

His slip at the gateway
remembered each time he approaches
Yes, it is painful.
His movement remains
towards the outside;
when ecstatic
things often stick together
do not always become unstuck
understands where
consciousness patterns the eventive.
Death becomes a high order he thinks
and hears when he falls: Freedom
doesn't break from the definity of solitude.

Buzzard

The Burglar's arm
lifts
its shadow expands and
disappears as pattern
leads to an edge of contradiction
fades out
sound of a wheel catching a blade
rising pitch as the edge approaches exactness
The arm carries a cloth wipes
a brow then the blade
eyes rapidly squint
to see it against sunshine
separate a drop of oil
despite the impression that surface tension
remains intact.

A prospectus defines
potential
lowers from the window
into mud
The Burglar
doesn't prevent his future
His dropped weight
a momentary peace.
My dizziness propels his
image into vertigo
a demonstration of falling
of human-as-if-beast
The rising arm
shifted the looseness of tonal
edge into an ambiguity
where the rain hit the pavement
in Blenheim Gardens but
not the grass by the windmill
In that fear of being fettered

to the swing there
in the mechanics of fall
an axial movement
from vertical to horizontal
yet fixed in alternations.

Embedded in such questions
of aspect
of perception
the Painter's arm turns a wheel
and her eyes watch the bed
move horizontally or the other arm
experiences the bed pull the blanket
flat as it moves away
from the pull and the
plate beneath bites the
paper, Then,
as the paper disappears from
the other side,
Then she noticed the plant   nettle
or samphire   crushed
under the rollers
watched it recover part of its shape,
after the bed released
it
at which moment
she had decided to let
the bed complete
its course and turned the
wheel again to free
the last leaves from the grip

Distant Gunfire   10.45   25.10.86
moves through the glass
holds attention

longer than after
its vibrations have
been absorbed
into debt and property.

The Burglar changes his shirt
and drops into
the garden without
weight until
his ankle twists
on broken surface.

Suddenly he sees someone
standing in the clearing.
There is no turning
back. The horizon
barbed wire
stapled to a wall
in the form of a double
helix.
He thinks of pouncing
the wire with his spare
shirt as a cushion and rejects
this. He feel invisible,
understands himself to be
inside a mask. He wonders
how it can be that his
flesh shivers on dry grass.

Bunny Hop

1.

Fifteen men came down the path
from the hut
stamped snowed shoes against
kerb stones and took
the day
in separate vehicles.
The Painter stood in Glanville Road
and watched the distant
gateway lock the atmosphere
Disquietened by her incessant howls,
she burns in her memory in her nervous
system in her eyesight
watched the Burglar kick at the gate
that would have opened at the touch
of his weakness.

2.

Progress from assumptions
of high symmetry and
equilibrium she set off
against local and far from perfect
order an irreversible growth
The process of patterning dust
cell-colonies   perception
things often stick together do not always
become unstuck
Ubiquitous in what is seen amorphous
The holes in structure comparable in size
with the canvas section itself
Her mark-making disordered not random
Long range correlations in the patterns
where distances far in excess of the forces

between them
describe tenuous objects
They scale elements of phase-transition physics
independent of the detail of interactions
on the iced-up window she had remembered
its viscous surface during growth
when some parts rearrange after sticking
find a more energetically favourable location.

3.

What a pleasure to walk the streets
when all that you love perpetuates
in which nobody could live and freely
beyond the norms and demands

At one slight bound the Burglar leapt
the verdurous wall
Lights on his feet
Then alone, as he supposed, all unobserved
unseen
his smell stealing the local distinctions
Weighed and weak
by his actions his
epistemological break
purely the notion of function
where input determines completely output—No,
not exactly—without memory—
No—without internal state—
No.

The Burglar's struggle against gravity
begins an irreversible vertigo
practised in a periodic and reversible fashion
otherwise the lure of his search of self

6.

Her bounce had to work
hard to cover up
what felt like
a heavy blow to the chest.
What I am about to say narrative
because interpretative
is this so?
Timedistance mediated
and because of my research into what
I interpret,
because of in addition memory perception imaginative
extrusions from what I interpret,
these overlapping histories of use
are part of the history of Brixton
whose needs they serve.

Under the trees by the windmill
the Bellman expels who looks back and who turns away.
Such values comply to the
nostalgic or memorative and beyond his ken.
I reduced earning power from other things besides art
She was more concerned to make work pay its way
part of this interest in the temporal
to deny any ownership of the residue of image making
class currency
day charts

Shrouds not paintings
Something simple and direct to act
as a residue for the images'
tactility
The whole process involved in the work
not only the resultant hangings

Any movement after tends to redefine
each image

The false impression
pre-empts the actual work itself
censored by misunderstanding

Time and again

a landscape of dust

memory and intention

The evidence of crime
and then the resultant image
criminality

Destruction of the image
as part of the healing
Undrawing erases the markings by
a cycle of body movements
materials space involvement

The Burglar came through the walkway
on a Go-cart
Yes
smashed the lock off
with a screwdriver and hammer
padlocked the letterbox
rearmoured the door
Yes
All the paintings were
turned to face the wall
Yes.

7.

Interpretation
a perceptual experience
The lightning or its flask
detected as an ordered temporal sequence
Psychophysical judgements
involved discrimination of the physical
parameters of each transient

It's hard to count verbally
Harder to replicate by motor output

The evidence for the absence of reportage
of tactility
her hands without scars
only memory

Fibronectin &c., mediates adhesion of neurones
acts with glycoproteins to provide a hierarchy of cues
that guide axons towards old synaptic sites
Structures become humanly visible
for debugging and analysis
and may be dumped

8.

Immune to stock market crash
the Burglar purchased a go-cart to roar the walkway
before the banks closed
A week later stolen
No immunity

Under the radicalism of the report committee
the tyranny of the majority

separated from the social contract
between private and public
that makes the value

Those begging by force
in an intense exchange of gesture
between comparative strangers
begin to fill the passageways

More than one clock runs on civilisation
There can never be one count down.

9.

It starts
that's right
Begins
Who are you
Eye bats through the net
in sun scatter
Still weightless
knowing the time briefly
before it is subsumed
in reflection

A musician talks about interpretation
equates loss of joy to speed
Balances structures of pitch and rhythm
built on tiny cells into patterns
moves one against the other
creates shifts, illusions of speed and space
'orgaismo' juxtaposes 'psicogramma'
translated as determined order against free,
functioning snapshots

I was honoured to be going 'up'
she said, which read as spiritual damnation
by my parents
They bring coal, tinned meat-and-vegetables,
and pullovers, in a homemade trunk
Restless on a staircase they watch
self-important attacking voices
of undergraduates training for criminality
They look through us towards 'better society'
My need for seclusion, as for food, restorative
against any State obligation to develop a detachment
or to see beyond depression and emptiness
To see the pointless liberation in used energies
where thuggery transcends class

10.

WHAT WE ARE SAYING IS THAT LOW-LEVEL RADIATION
CAN AFFECT THE BODY'S IMMUNE SYSTEM

ON HOT DAYS WE PACK INTO THIS HUT LIKE DUCKS
ON A VIDEO POND
WE LOOK DOWN TO ANOTHER LAYER UNDERNEATH
PACKED INTO LIGHT BOXES
She peels the tract from the mirror
WAR FILLS CERTAIN FUNCTIONS ESSENTIAL TO THE
STABILITY OF OUR SOCIETY; UNTIL OTHER WAYS OF
FILLING THEM ARE
DEVELOPED, THE WAR SYSTEM MUST BE MAINTAINED —
AND
IMPROVED IN EFFECTIVENESS

Under weightlessness
her stomach-felt acceleration questions

the biochemical clock
She slumps into the array of flowers and roars

11.

I hoped that it would not be used
and trembled
I was desperately anxious to find out
if its intricate mechanism would work
These were dreadful thoughts I could not help

Last few second/Stand ahead/Now!/burst of light/
         deep growl/explosion/relaxed relief

Just when it appeared settled came a flask
The top was settling and boiled
Upward and then earthward
It freed itself from its stem
floated with tremendous speed
a mountain of jumbled rainbows
Bewilderment turned into pride
The grass started dying
a crimson-purple glare
Burrowed into the ground
like a blazing rabbit.

12.

Vernal delight and joy
able to drive all sadness
but despair
A physicist sat on a jeep bonnet played drums
towards pain and misery

IF THE WELFARE OF SOCIETY INSTEAD OF BUILDING ON

EXTRAORDINARY EXERTIONS BECOMES REASONABLY
ORGANISED
THE NEED OF GREAT ABILITIES DIMINISHES
THE PERMANENT POSSIBILITY OF WAR
REMAINS THE BASIC SOCIAL SYSTEM
IN WHICH THE INSISTENCE ON GREATNESS
PERPETUATES ITS GRIP

The painter turns to the window
In the distant garden the Burglar
limps over a field of dust
The mathematical biology of paradise's low
fractal dimension could amplify noise
or self-affine
It could aggregate with cluster-cluster from
cognition and fluff
Zero surface tension sources noise
in the discrete arrivals of potential happiness

She turned back to her canvas
I effected qualitative changes in habit
Factured a conflict.   Symmetry and
anisotropy, ordering space and noise.
Gradually I consider the scale of dominance
that effected this.

Buzzard Glide

Early in morning staple
snapped the defences
Hysteresis as a function
of the Burglar's constitution
relates his transgressions
across public and private
There's something about the
initial state of her appearance, her
arrival, that embodies the memory of
recent past just as the pattern
of magnetisation gives a clue to
local repositories of events
to be smeared out
by the extreme conditions
of her arrival in his perception.
Specified variations in his DNA
led to differences in his
felt experience; wavelengths differed
according to the protein component in his
rod and cone cells
The photopigment embedded in the infolded
membrane of his receptors, initiated electrical signals
from absorbed light
His nerves find the ratio of
quantum catches in different classes of cone and
regenerate images of the past
His mimesis thus prescriptive
rather than imitative
Concerned with those constitutional deletions
which overlap a cluster of separate but closely
linked genes that pattern the development of
the kidney, iris, and urogenital tract.

In one example, the Burglar took
skin fibroblasts from a householder which he fused

with hamster cells using polyethylene gycol
and selected hybrid clones
in an atmosphere supplemented in the garden
by fetal calf serum and ouabain.
These hybrid colonies were expanded and
recloned through the mains water
experienced eventually in both general,
and in details, as toxic rainfall.

He looks up to see the figure again, to
assess the pattern of its arrangement,
to recognise it.
His inhibition as he does this partly
enhances the tuning of
his orientations.
Knowing where he is encourages knowing what it
is that confronts him.
She sees him as apparitor and bawd;
as if from nowhere
yet here to exploit her.
Beekeeper with emphasis on returns;
on the idea of feed her sugar, then
smoke her out.

She drops a tract on late Triassic
tetrapod distributions
revised according to per-taxon extinction rates
punch-carded against
the palaeomagnetic signal carried
by thermo-remnant rocks.
The Burglar locks in his data regarding
chromosome 11 halotypes determined by
the segregation of restriction alleles in
somatic cell hybrids.
Mass extinction may represent a significant

departure from the background rates,
but it events in equally timed space.

Reflecting on the obscurity
of this image the Burglar begins an
analysis of his judgement
and its relation to interpretation;
the discrimination of the physical
parameters of each transience
What in the fleeting was hard
to count, harder still to
replicate, because of an absence
evident without tactile sensation.
To put it differently
the condition probability
that what he saw existed
relied on his confidence.
In order to analyse and thus
orient by patterns of polaroid skylight
all he needed was an array
of receptors, a template, to
scan and match the patterns
in the cosmos.

All the while I feel my fit
my joy stand upside down for it.
And still the farther off from her
Dear Sight I am, the readier
As she emerges from the frottage she
projects that which sees itself in him
from the patterns in the spat-on wall.

Bumble Bee

Fatigued by his attempt
to reach
Blake falls in Kennington Road
before a half-open gateway
Puts into question
the subjectivity of weight;
prevents its gather.
She falls and rotates about
a canvas on the floor
there tries a variety
of orientations
for hanging it.

What is positive in Blake's weight
sinks
Held on while losing
his balance, or the Painter
becomes vertigo
felt as insinuation
finds herself over a void. It breaks
open an absence of place.
A mirror fastened across the posts of the gateway. No,
it's not a mirror, it must be an
effect of the light.

She stretches out of Repose
and lifts from a couch
Their bodies are not clarified as
arrivals of consciousness.
Understanding,
perhaps made of sensations,
events in patterns of connectedness
that constitute it, which
give their processes recognition exposed
to fields of sensations,

can change the connectedness
without altering the emphasis of
the pattern.

Their experience of materiality not lost.
Not lost and persists
given duration,
like but not actually
eternity, Not yet immobilised by malnutrition,
simply jags of pain from toxics
that prevent some movements.

In different angles, weathers, the colours move,
the reflections suggest, light from greens
then from blacks.
Inscriptions made by gains of momentum
underfoot in the walkway pansied mosses
checkerboard the right of way.
I am irremissible, as if free
with respect to the past, but
birdcaged watch the flight
outside. I breathe the gravity
of where I am. It is not
the ballast of hereditary weight;
I weigh *myself*.
Never long anguished by things done
stricken by what has not been.
Memory doesn't
replace the felt the paving stone
unless relieved in
some temporary anæthesis
or complete relaxation.

From vertiginous heights to a sludge
her arrogance breaks the gate

Humiliation by the windmill
at the next curve of the switchback, blinks.
At each section different attributes
of the image, intensity colour space.
Each switch reduces her metabolic requirement
doubles her dynamic range.
In the reflections diffidence
fragmented into abstraction and thoughtlessness

until the balance locks
awash in shadows and noise, the heterochrony
of existence as the suspended cage
swings.
Blake's fatigue
gave his momentum gain
unseated his load
His shock from quick recovery
greater than the effect of his fall.

3. Civic Crime

Cakewalk

The image of a woman frottaged
by the Burglar
to the wall shifts
with his attention reads
a bicontinuous sponge
with surfactant interfaces.

His cleansing gaze as he sees it
rapidly fluctuates the curvature
of her shapes. They begin to leave
the wall and spatter
the footpath.
The Informer's report confirms

they are metallic balls of
crystalline liquids sandwiched
in saliva honeycombs and
dynamically disordered into droplets
disturb the gravel.
Oh what a wonderful world.

Tries to stop it and cannot.
The variety of their phase behaviour
encourages a focus deception
His long range spatial ordering
fantasises a language progression
from colloidal fluids to crystals.

Their viscosity reminds him of impact prints
left on an exit window by his fingers
stained with damaged plant cells
traced in the virus templated,
the Informer notes, as a leukaemia copy
in one of the collagen gene's first introns.

There can be no question of wipe-out.
The gravity-induced sedimentation
of the image in its suspensions had
stabilised the Burglar knew it
in the language of the City's
sintered adhesion.

Simultaneously he holds court
in The Prince of Wales
traps concentration
rather than solitude
A single organisation
of informers feeds
the evidence mode

in the dole queue
at one standing pours
three pints into his head
Such lethean measure
lures
the material electro-chemistry
of his abandon.

He chooses to ignore any digital alternatives
Speaks of life in terms of wealth:
his nerves scan the City as its temperatures
pass the red index limits lighting the Brixton horizon
His neuronal evolution capitalises on the spatial separation
of proteins in the synapses of his cellular processes.

Away from the perinuclear destruction
in his cell bodies
to the subterranean horizon,
his holdings are achieved by macromolecular stabilisation:

a vocabulary trench
almost voided of the means to dredge.

Intricate spreads of nerve cell processes
spatially
separate
and immunise his semiological remittance
from
the expression of his pragmatic turnover.

Innocence avoids complacent
isolation because he didn't know
the quest. Singularity
relieved of all responsibility
because he is a fool
run by terror, nothing
whatsoever taken seriously.

All day toxics
the narrative in its transparent
cruelty in an effort
not to become what I behold
but a stalwart attitude
to sustain a disciplined day
does not dissipate inner shudder.

Return
to a Faraday cage
dizzy from the static
metal escalator
on the down slope
defines
incompleteness.

He lives in fear of breakdown,
in sensitivity of capture.
His skid turns from the calm,
austere garden
back to the consequences of
the City's transcendence of its glow.

He cannot teach himself
to ignore the
screams and riot outside
but evades approaching darkness in both
the garden and the City move against him
Explosion

Feels like shatter,
you thought, Feels like
implosion of perfection
made of itself.
He watches himself
gaze at his abandon
birefringent on the footpath.

A plantal condition of Beauty
a transient flower
which he stoops to pluck
The difficult
capable of depth without
a weighty solution
against reflection.

Having what is essential without
having enough
limits of desire and thus the image:
a ceasing of hope couples to a ceasing of fear.

The two of them struggle
in front of the local nightsafe.

As he watches he participates in desire transformed in greed
oriented so that what he sees occurs in the direction he looks
at the moment it happens.
The distance of its occurrence from him
measures the same rest framed memory of the image
such that all other components vanish.

Necessity, weight, value condition
but do not constitute
the work
what do you do?
he is asked,
Why didn't you
sign on last week?

Sailing on a mirror
with birds in front of him
he scans for a
boop tone
to check his idealism and its concomitant
realist aesthetic.

To balance out the arguments for leaving well alone
the Mathematician acts now to prevent inflationary overheating.
The breakdown problem
of established intellectual frameworks for answering questions
begins at the apple tree precisely at five o'clock in
the afternoon ransacked the edges of innovation.

A reverberant repression
tunes results from interactions
which cannot be separately attributed.

Precise connections between
similar colour responses activate
specific connections between orientation responses.

Look at it! produces
a stimulus constellation.
Gunfire, 11.00 p.m., 17th July
His nerves image
labile charts
which change with use.

The image of a finger tip
in the Informer's somatosensory cortex
expands after a period of intense stimulation
encroaching by up to one millimetre
into zones normally occupied by the rest
of the finger and part of the hand.

The slender phase partition
separates the successful making of a solvent for stains
from the deadly compound which explodes at a touch.
"Hitherto I have preferred to endure toxics on
my fingers rather than run the risk of being
forcibly expelled through the window."

Neurons overlap receptive fields
are modulated by the angle of gaze
the strength of the responses to the image
at a particular location on the retina
varies according to the relative positions of
his eyes.

A topological image is not required
to get the readout of spacetime.
The neurons in the Burglar's facility

learn the association between
eye and retinal positions.
His neuronal operations are probabilistic.

This perception
results from continual cross-reference
amongst a variety
of stolen properties.
The activity in one is shaped
by that in others.

In the garden projections from two areas converge in a third.
They do not overlap but terminate in adjacent patches.
His single perception of her appearance explodes
from specific ensembles of neurons
located in several pockets each responding
to a particular feature of the stimulus field.

He stands imbecilic
to report what he sees.
The depth of his endurance
an index of his necessity.
His balm is a wonder whack more often than sunlight.
To be everywhere is to be negatively capable in loss.

The accident rapidity
took an age to occur and happened
quickly
proportions exactly
mixed into synthesis in the chamber
received pressure mass then noticed
it was not implosion-screened.

His language response a free mirror
stimulated by sensations of distance separation

from a second free mirror and produces a
permanent deformation in a gravitational
wave-burst with memory
in which the waves stores the signal forever.

A possibility the author turns
away thinks no one else has to approach
the discovered gasp of appearance
as if persuaded by anticipation of sex
he leans toward
its ephemeral image embossed on the wall.

The investigation, the movement
in the trap of unconcern
That Paradise became a prison (unreadable)
shines to some
marigold my hands scarred from burns
of its perfected collective
its hypergolic shock.

No warning
no preparation had made
resistance possible
it simply happened inside
a joy it happened
and broke pieces
into less than recognition.

As she focuses
the Photographer comes to something
which to her is Beauty
and stops there
instead of winding the lens
into acuity

This delay
requires memory of the image spacetime
and facility for discerning difference
These requirements, maps in the premotor cortex
One deals with the plan and initiation of actions
the other with their guidance and execution.

If the Burglar could take
a light rest without insouciance
what he found
incompatible with the garden spacetime
Some wild bird
a sensation smelt
as it lifted from the flower bowl

decided about what is essential
and had excitement
what is enough pleasure jaded
towards holocaust. No more disasters
no catastrophes no more dissension
Only resignation
All accounted for.

Turned to face the bark and tears
limited desire to cure fear
unchains prisoner from escort
influx from correspondence
gazing from grasping
severs threads
of silken tackle.

I make a broken delivery of the business
as I become intelligent
take a slack on a
reward risk ratio:

not free
and not forever.

Processes continually modify
my feedback and lateral interactions.
An ecology that rabbits biologically
impoverished situations
where the cortex becomes a map of the world
each sensory modality charts several spacetimes in

different runabouts with about a dozen images
of the visual suspensions and half a dozen each of
the auditory inputs and how it feels.
It is functions that are mapped:
single areas contain multiple trace groups
bursting in different dimensions.

The Engineer's nonsense
dispenses with
misogynist fantasy.
He watches behind closed flesh
Doors of incredulous gaze
screen an unfolding
elliptic umbilic.

Spat at the wall
at loneliness
through fragments into
loss of description
dizzy from static, you cry,
What was that?
withdrawn from my own affairs in particular.

I switch on the cage
Cells selective for wavelength are among

those selective for orientation.
On the footpath the Bikeboy separately notes
size, shape, colour, position and direction of movement
with one glance.

Mottling leaves the garden wall
becomes marble after marble
breaks the working
glass an intensity of pressures
stronger than hail
and rolling on impact.

Their similarity of direction
marks out a field of gravity
beyond the garden wall
Exclusive doors conceal a haze indexed yellow
Marble-pillared,
leather-bound, pieds-a-terre.

The City's policy
whiteballed to ensure the Informer
runs into the right kind of people
Always a light flashing somewhere
Everybody is very tired
Earning a fortune

Desire and greed are matched
in a "she looks beautiful" eugenics
A chain of electro-chemical reactions
summarises into
the will to keep up standards

An order to establish
an options exchange encourages favour
forces a go out produces the

image futures
without sites that could lend
such aspirations considered cohesion.

Camel Walk

The Photographer's image of the Burglar
separates in her nostrils
begins to heave
as he loses his marbles
When you know the smoke above the town
you know where you are
When you love the culture of where you are
you love the world
Towards the end of our life here
decidability clarified.

The proof based on the idea that
all that was possible to construct
capable of simulating others
produced a halting problem
Whether there actually would be
a stop or an eternity.

The plan was once to define
sequence as a whole number
expressed rather
arranged
as increasing numerical order
Each program assigned its output data
a diagonal run of this table
changing and the new run becomes
an unlisted number
corresponds to the output
of no computer program whatsoever

You compare the state of presence
with fragments of what might have been
a middle disposition
or is it virtuosity's arrogance
at odds with the known the fraudulent

a sublime smoothness
dipped into an expected prism
a measured vortex
trammed with a cold finger.

In this rhetoric disquisition
the grisaille creed
frames each memory rose
stiffened by an old gas pipe
or the sensibility shifts
to command an older typeface
pestilence   the many coloured smile
your breath fills my body
leaves me without desire.

But not blame exactly. The process
of vitality entrammelled in code
believing the promise
of presence, the optimum
spin of immunological certainty
where the good is prescribed
oblivious to greed
you begin your weight check
a simplicity that cannot be demonstrated.

The mixture of vertiginal
with lateral consequence or what
was struggled to achieve now sold
You steal the day and sell the night
unsure which is which
No wonder or turn towards the marvellous
Only toxic hysteria
raves into homeorhesis
until oblivion confirms what you wanted.

The image of your desire
snookered or shadowed
by its own presentiment
Old as the industrial tip
trampled over on the way
home from another yard run
Beauty and Perfection interchange
Forgotten almost at the instant
of synapse before perception.

Vigour and concentration
tangled in muscle traction
crushed beneath cell clots
into the equivalent of barking dogs
randomised by alarms throughout
the walkway as the trees are removed
The Fireman burns them with
hot wires and cage saws
adding the furniture from a skip on top.

The horizon lights up or
at least glows and a
row of us stand and watch
one last time before
our lease runs out
There's not much point but
some record this and hold
on to the balcony rails
to earth their tempers.

The learned thieves gather at
the Windmill and eat chocolate molluscs
Their calling is given reverence
When you join them the sky
is nearly dark but you call it

morning. You exchange open framed
mutation with a view to improve
the conditions indexed by an
ability to tell the time without external source.

I watch my own image burning
and melting until the globs
of my presence dissipate down the
footpath towards the
firing chamber. The gully
that empties everytime I swallow
and fills with your stench
The City men meet you there
and switch baskets.

There now everything is sacred
except rest and the pound at
the door echoes or repeats
until the sound has no discernible
break. Vigour becomes the only virtue
power-leaded into every microwave
plant until saturation is sanctioned
Stamped onto each window hatch
with the photograph of a mammal.

At last anyway it's just about over.
You break me apart before
the first shocks are recognised
The pressure build has been too slow
to purchase. Almost without
notice I leave the garden
and stay at once
There is nothing I can about it
There is nothing **to** do.

Cha Cha

The Mathematician considers the Artist
brings together in his eyes
an understanding of agitated cubes
to release
the Artist's mystical view of heavy water.
I do not know what I am
when I hate the destroyer of when I am
I hate street speak
Away from beginning my death there
without decision—fogged.

There's a lack of air under your impact theory:
none that can postulate impossible to take part
incapable of thinking becoming another colloquium
destroyed in a let-go solution.
Without this idealisation
a continual stop.

The guesses were not many to scramble
phased in fractions
decoded without
disarray
decreasing alphabetic disorder.
Some supposed you roughly dissipated input noise
or a squared blockage of that position.
Static and the old walk prevents
a listed code
Exclusive, away from the input,
the now unplanned computer.

I ignore a loss of situation
clustered of this presence, filling out
a frenzied prevention
or without ability, simplicity's generosity
fixed without knowing a truth.

A blasé roughness
lifted out of an unexpected cloud
Approximation spread loosely
flooded without a hot digit.

Out of that stated quiet
the collage unspecified
breaks some ashes of amnesia
loosened into a new electric cable.
Not the felt either. The skin tightens
to deny suggestion newly embossed with
joy. Your few blackened grimaces,
my inhaling, empties your grasp and
approaches you with fulfilment.

The cause around and about the fixed
without complaisance. The gates decode
studied lies
of absence. The minimum
still a vulnerability.
When is not decoded
awareness giving
the stop suspension
A complexity that could have given value.

The horizontal precipitates
with vertical random or when,
not rested, to prevent the purely sensible,
I give night and buy the day
to ensure my status
Turn your mundane
into healthy movement
calmed in the muscles
now against what I disliked.

The blankness my saturance.
Openness lit
your decision into
a new natural hollow
untouched without
visit. That open staleness coded as
noise I read as imperfection held onto
Remembered then and after
in unseen disconnection.

Your complaisant spread
loosened a cluster of
growing particles gravitated
out of the still sound of absence
organised without bells
A spaciousness the clearing fills.
You engineer with
cold field glue
subtracting towards a loaded uncertainty.

The nearness down or
spread without
ignition seeing
many continuals in front of
your face in
This line not
one forgotten and released
off of planes elevated
to calm sky.

The ignorance in your artifice splits
and spits rice husks
or listens to the taken obviousness
Where I earth the
distance I do not speak

but hold onto closure. Any
stability to demolish
the potential haphazard in this
inability. The space with internal emptiness.

I ignore blank evaporation
And adhere the field
out of your absent coagulation upon the
meadow the
squenching the ridge
This fullness, sometimes, you spit
and empty my sweetness
The Garden I
unlock.

Here then, cannot be irrelevance
Always active the tap in
the wall when singular
now unheard
Repairs prevent the many vices you code
as a resistant macro-particle clasped or
positioned into the rant that cannot be disagreed with
and lifts the reinforced wall
without using animation.

Soon always exactly continues.
I mend your traces
the many misses that cannot be comprehended.
The release has not been fast enough
to sell some of the shares
and I missed your arrival in the City
I go to often.
Here nothing can be avoided.
Here everything gets done.

Charleston

The Physicist imagines how
            his world will be
before he becomes part of its process
            Through a recognition
of similar structures in his organs
            to those of his companion's
he projects the potential
            of his capabilities' achievement

She lifts out of fear the Painter
            in a stopframe spacetime
levitated there
            in a serenity
clutches legs beneath her
            forms an ovoid held
with an asymmetry to the head
            proud of the curvature

He tries to follow
            uses a pole to push up
towards the occupied spacetime
            shakes on one arm on the pole end
as his body lifts into the
            periphery of her position
but cannot manage
            the frame held obvention

His formula based on four experiments
            and an assumption
Presumed force between circuits
            acted on a line between them
a force between the two elements
            presumed to be equal and opposite
loses the comprehension of the law's reliance
            on the completeness of the system

I am sensible of my crime
                but cannot abhor it
Duty, honour, virtue
                no longer inform
I am not yet a monster
                but frail
I am not without mutation
                but natural

Levels of confidence
                produce an almost horizontal line
but predict a sudden
                drop
No-drop maintenance
                encouraged by
one of the promoters
                whilst others gave attention

but anticipated an exhaustion
                from facial contortion
anticipated overeagerness
                on the part of promoters
as gestures of perfection
                enlarge out of proportion
and the Gravatt's dumpy leveller
                reduces the iridium assizes

Had he assumed no energy radiation
         and allowed for the field effects
between acceleration and charge
         the Painter notes
he might have understood
         that his own inertia
 on his tendency
         to conserve

Charley-Bop

The Informer held precision high
and that continues
Any notion of biological interaction
can be discounted
The beat of gentleness
if that wasn't completely supposition
was not apparent. The skin's heat
anyway lost in its sient entity
its rank reindividuation.

Frenzy was recoded as foreign matter,
in a low fractal dimension,
repressed in syntactic exactitude
in which the lawless become recognised
in the blur record associated with the image
Self-control that now included
a filling-out of consciousness
subsumed all coding
in an active decision about categories.

The image of concrete purpose
became the cue
without question
of the empirical failure of value
No redoubting
continued discount of the distressed
The applause in the face of tyranny
sanctioned by codes of heritage
and the strong arm.

The promise of peace
addressed as control
any complaint that risk
must be avoided and
involved stamping out wilful freedom

in those that would better be served
as children
They screech through the
tunnel at Monument underground

Held by tweezers of laser light
inside a blinding sandwich
where depth perception of what good it does
gets decided by investors' returns.
Whilst back here the plants die
from an over-emphasis on cultivation
where all filth and foul iniquity
demands that the earth be burnt
And rules insist that the danger is necessary

But what it leads to isn't considered
an innocence discarded by the despair of wealth
This stuff will not do
The fit is without synaptic reciprocation
No understanding wends towards pretence
of comprehension. Sure there's a way
out—it's called Exile
I plant a row of boxhedge cuttings
and retire to a barbed enclosure

Straps of duty are now replaced
with predetermined measure
signified by a piercing code
accounted without consciousness
The rigour of its dispensation
dependent on its spectrum of sorting
deals amongst phenotypes on a genetic basis
in an ongoing populating of ecosystems
in which the ideal is fixed yet unknown
and power oppresses others of their kind

The Informer leaves the irriguous tunnel
to reorganise the sorting
He returns to the shrine
hung from his driving mirror
to the explosion in my ears
from the throat box
black trains pass through the nerve gas
of the vibrating City
scrambled into summer's
realignment of moisture.

He reports two genes located in different translational
reading frames with one end of a **gag**
overlapping the end of a **pol**:
site-directed mutagenesis and amino-
acid sequencing localises the site of
frameshifting to a codon near the end of the
overlap. This was trapped against
an averaged autocorrelation function
and an unresolved reference star
after subtraction of a near-gaussian seeing component

The close similarity between the
two reports demonstrates, he noted,
the lack of any resolution in the images
In the former an out-of-frame
configuration left a genomic dread in situ
the latter had been dominated
by a photon-spike and carried assumptions
of a black-body spectrum,
blue shifts of the trough, and a
constant velocity since the explosion.

He opened the boot of his car to let the alarm out
and set up an optical trap at power levels

What explosion? sufficient to give manipulation at
high velocity. The orientation of individual cells
in space was achieved using a pair of "single-
beam gradient force traps" to give the
dominant component a push
of dielectric particles into the high-intensity
region of the focus. High-resolution
viewing allowed him to hold the image
at each of its ends and orient it at will.

As he came down from Jebb Avenue
he produced a viscous drag
It instigated a vertically hung clump
and tipped into the viewing plane
Truth went out the window
In his lap a diagram of burglary
He had nothing to express and little
to think about, the place had been cased
But where does that get us?

He was inclined to pull the brakes on thinking
when looking at risk
He operated the quiet trap slowly
without interest in knowing its aesthetics
always accurate, always unhappy
The sound of complaints, pessimism, a dripping faucet
timing a moment of strain a difficult waiting
before he reached the Thames
his face had swollen with weeping.

Turn back, his voice said
You travel all in vain
He pulls the wheel on the right
hits the gate
The image bursts onto his windscreen

fills the car with solutions
let out as he recedes
A rush of instances without application
It is not worth discussion in detail.

The vertical drop linked regions of different
elasticities. The crash shifted
the demand curve and settled at the
break point. Oligopolistic behaviour
varied from collusion to almost
perfect competition. Such a phase
shift prevented ideal focus.
Generosity to enemies betrays friends, a social
fitness dependent on a known polis.
A vertical drop that displays a horizontal
shelf of marginal revenues.

Chicken

The misogynist produces now
                    a soiled history
before he becomes part of its process
                    Through inhibition
of similar structures in his organs
                    to those he is disgusted by
he erects the parental
                    crack of his hatred

The subject shifts outer fiat
                    inwards shot from a pace climb
regulated stare
                    inner perversity
fetches a crushed beatitude
                    normalised instead
withers assimilates to feed
                    proud of the curvature

He flies to borrow
                    fuses a toil twistor
affords peroxide pace climb
                    fakes onomatopoeia the toil bends
accesses commodity thrifts
                    perpetuity over perdition
buttered damage
                    the same shell invention

His form based on faulty acidity
                    and consumption
Presumed force between circuits
                    fractured spacetime
a force between two elements
                    presumed to be subjected and subjector
poses the tension of the claw's pliance
                    on the screen of wisdoms

I am spent of my crime
                   but cannot judge
what I owe to my virtue
                   elongated and sawn
I am wanted amongst her
                   but male
I am weighed and muted
                   but not real

Gazelles of fidelity
                   juiced and most presentable
of dereliction a sudden
                   crop
to stop brain sense
                   cabbaged by
the voters and the voters'
                   hilted intention

Fut cruciated angle hoist
                   foam racial torsion
dissipated over eagles
                   of the shaft ropes
as guests of transgression
                   barge out on propellant
and the gravity bumps the antelope
                   juiced in radium seizures

Plaid and grooms fin lock
                   and crowd for the weald decks
even acerbic and labour
                   the subject floats
what had stood
                   bone of inenarrable
lies bending
                   to serve

4. Dispossession & Cure

Dirty Dog

There then direct perception
all sources assessment or evaluations
of truth
Behind the red leathered chair
a black radiator
In the canteen *Cambridge Collage*
by Robert Motherwell
The only other graphic a
reproduction of Jackson Pollock's
Autumn Rhythm on the jurors' waiting
room wall

This ease and shabbiness and content
(I in my new dress)
rather formidable

I feel a prodigious weight
which I can't lift yet
Several problem at once
The greenhouse began to be built.

Passing our own limits
to tell the future
It occurred to me last night
I would merge all interjected
passages and end with solitude
or confinement
as choice

LONDON JANUARY '89–HEREFORD JULY '89

Choo Choo

What accounts for the Bellman's condition
superimposed accelerated accumulation
Toxic metals in his vertebrate frame
trace the reply
regarding social danger

His oracle quickly stated
Crown over portcullis and chains
counter-read as a smudge of lipstick
on handwritten envelope
carefully posted with a complex of
white floral fragrance with tuberose and jasmine
top notes on a chypre and spicy background
Gets up the nose

The toxicity of mobilised metals
exceeds the total van load
of radioactive and organic wastes
measured by the beer needed to dilute them
The Bellman's drinking water
fraught with influence without modification
anticipates abandon read in the tumbler

A second genetic code remains largely undeciphered
his structure of enzymes coupled each amino acid
to an appropriate transfer in his molar fillings
His language both non-degenerate and Ah! Bellman!
More deterministic than a frozen accident

What what courage and fortune overlap provide
scales of or on the top edge of a garden fence
Hi! there! decisions between gravity and entropy

produce call it a drawing
after an essential repair of neuron
restitution but not reversal

The probabilities of his processual kinetics accords
a knowing that cannot exclude the uncertainty of its frame
On his cart most obstacles to complete
mixing are incomplete
There is no automatic spread fag
fag even if the shape of it horseshoes
rather than elliptically poxes

The visualisation of his future
Ah the fluid thought mixes fatigue
distinguishes chaotic trajectories
Who make the rules need to know disorder well
Different patterns do not necessarily work
the satisfaction in different ways

It's proof that the Umpire sits in pain
holds the balance
a metallic mouth speaks
openly astride the main shaft
oil warms gained by the mass in its fall

A collapsed transgression recites to a stenographic fix
a hum in the Bellman's ear
encourages a different mixture
merges panic
with a drawn down squareness or
what they were becomes what they appear to be
machines spinning his resounding bell

A figure called Success drops from his tailboard
holds a dish in righthand

in left an ear of metallic corn and dead poppies
The condition arrives at attunement as it moves through
broken quarry stones in the forecourt of Granvile arcade
plastic leaves blown from turbulent warnings
touched by the hand as it is taken away
from asking its question

Chug

Turned the drivel on
gave shape
at seven in time
ceremonies
to find them capping
turns into stone
the pox and they
embodies life force
have another man-flight
Night belongs
in orbit
to the animals
takes us out
strikes a stone
of modernism into
a cough syrup painting
against cloud
things
seem to go
wrong
but it doesn't answer what
the hand asks
Simply a figurative use of autumn
juxtaposed an account in Virgil
probably disparate won't do
and an image of what might have
that precedes what does it
precede

To the Analyst anger
signifies love
and an enclosure that
has veno-gated
part of the same piccess

eiclaved in emblematic
self-consci
i an f e

2

To the Analyst anger
signifies love
and an enclosure that
has venom-gated
part of the same process
enclaved in emblematic
self-consciousness
in and for itself for another
into dissolves of aptness
unique spins of privacy in
neoteric dark
slam boarded on
the judder ride before
dawn breaker the synapse.

Each judgement
the Analyst determines
rests with a war lord
in the process of signature
on the blower
Eh—at the flagged desk
Right? sparks of decision
Don't he—about the next
genetic aspiration
on a fresh blotter
tough enough to take
before the chafe removes clarity
ratification
the next hyperpyrema
rateable values
decided by auscultation

3

My probe reports
anxiety flushed out with
on accordance
a pocket calculator
in which harmony
cross-paged with the oracle
is not one of the options
gives an oil deficit
after a wheeze index
adjudication of reason
against brain damage.

Such exhibition supersedes the otherness
of freedom of itself
construction and composure
a supersession of ambiguity
related to a becomes certain
a moralistic of itself
Net loss proceeds to supersede
useful energy its own self
a perpetual motion
the other that is itself

in which machines
are imperfectly efficient

In a spacetime of fear
the Analyst does not relent
before distress and bondage
of almost universal some call human leverage
True to me in my uncertainty
raised to thought it despises
appeals to the eye
given itself to plunges
by methodical deprivations
of images indulges
to a full rigour
exercises in negative impression
the shadowy existence
fills a blue-grey sedge
between the eyes.

This indicates
notes the Analyst
that strange cough coupling
of the undeciphered genetics
and the use of portcullis and
chains on the front of the
ledger the broken seal rewaxed
with intoxicant

chorus Hook

whistler-mode
choruses accompanied
by high-frequency bursts
electrostatic noise visualised from
studies of wideband plasma wave data
made from spacecraft correlates with continuum radiation

at those bursts the chorus band displays hook-like shapes
window panes covered on the outside a harmonic
structure they say apparently results from the
burst intensity modulated at the
frequency of the
chorus

chreod

WHERE THE PATHWAY OF CHANGE IS CANALISED MEMORY AND
PERCEPTION A HARMONIC STRUCTURE APPARENTLY RESULTS

cigar

in spatially-homogenous visualisation where matter is
dynamically negligible near the singularity a small spatial region
which is spherical at some time becomes infinitely long and thin
as time moves towards calm and the surface area to volume ratio
increases towards a cigar

Circle

> Opposite
> To the right
> the end of the passage
> straight
> through the formalities
> coming back
> There's no particular
> back
> like this
> in the end
> careful
> come back to
> turn
> unexpected

No angel speaking
at a future
get fat on reserve and modesty
a nation's curse
from the summits
Evermore
an oligarchy bribed
And no one marvels
You weep and write
broken with strain
crazed
with calm footing
this is the crime the curse
prospers

the telephone
and the passage
the front door
rest and chorisis
back
at the
phone
things are possible
no reason why
But possible
things
In the end
broke through
the end of another war
extraordinary
expected lies
and coming back

Sadness corrosive within
speaks
low in your ears
the tramp of progress
drives
conscience tradition and name
explodes the science of
predation and blame
refrains from witnessing
your flag
in the soil recoil
in the rag of your curse
and its burst
of patriotic complacence

She wonders if she
will burn the paper

After the storm
at our feet
the post in the passage
Having been anxious as
well as having appeared so
Outside the gate
question everyone
the cleaner
the postman
The answer repeats
I don't know
I don't know anything.

Conga

Gathered at the nation's sickbed
evenin sky owered onto
yellow irises through daffodils
mimosa into street lanterns
lowers into plasticisers on
the face of an SAS officer as she
approaches the supermarket
Oh Hereford evening Oh absent
healing satellite warning
burst into jump jet schizophrenic
peace warming the panes beneath
the greenbacked lawn

I stood half naked on the verge
partly exposed my genital
photographer sent the proofs
to the agency back into a post
bag the size of passive management in the
wind-up co-operative proceeds from moves
into burnt a paperpoint institution a
dressing the rules towards portfolio bonding

meet to discuss the phenomena
evident points to climatic
buzz-phrases resonation urgentics
disrupt the fragile bank
balcony
intelligibility overlaps language for
people whose hearts are heated moving towards
restriction overlaps with purity
a folk taxonomy uniform or informant

the cosmology in recent gossip
environment itself as hazard
themes of Nature and Art in the ceiling
indicate what was stored below in cabinets
appearances release memories
of what is hidden
Bertold the Black identified
manufacturing ballistics
to the left the results are tested
by means of a catapult bomb hurlers
against the Danes in 1354

freedom here becomes bitter
loss of hope
the emptiness that follows
creates no memory
I can't remember what was eaten
it was black and soft
patronised by collaboration
keeping comparatively healthy
saves me from despair
lunches are the worst part of memory
closed doors and friends knocking
existentialists who become policemen
corroborated by fear
by certainty
opens the briefcase
takes out a portcullis and a pair of chains
I'm not rembling
I'm tired of trembling

A close integrity relates
events, acts, roles and genres
and the configuration processed
In each curing event the speech act of the
special knower produced in western distortion
the doctor's prescription

Continental Walk

In full voice sent cooked in rice in leek water
to fight for nation
they wont be singing   walked
when they come back
enforced inactivity
at a time when nothing
but action could make sense   on soft red earth
civilisation on the operating   banks of the Wye
table we sit in the waiting   and the Frome
room neither pity nor hope policing
what begins in routine policing invented new curry
hardens into preservation   using leeks and frageolets
                          yellow curry orange carrot brown
                   cumin black pepper   with green pepper shifted with
        and Albers   in Chevreaul Newton Goethe   researching colour
   Pictorial art guided by a   shifting to the luxury of bathing naked eventually
rhythm of structures to which consonant weight   of colours
   after investigation of immediacy   should correspond
      we think sex is alright   and spontaneity

Nature and Art in this together suit
to Make of the parts towards a wise aim
Calm extents of many intellectual domains
reinforced an aristocratic candour
Deeply wounded rather than embittered
To enmity and disappoitment opposed
many different constructions and great industry
marshalling them for common sense, so said, triumph
An expression of tenderness patience and health

The choice from appearances impersonal exactitude
express harmoniously a state of mind concurrently
depdendence on Nature depreciates those who
would paint without example relativity of tonal
values in which the number claculations affect the eye

[198]

The equation between rupture
from the earth and aesthetic
decision in which geometry
and number express the amplitude
of love To embrace each particular
Agitation borrows the broad arc
of calm Colour sense enraptures
form an involucre of outwardness

The nation's life as outward
state to which all activity
aspires as death see to be
a calm separation given nausea
by the pressure of each damaged
lung Common sanity now alien
without reciprocation in love
appositions seize the muscles
of the heart It's incredibly
easy to die so much harder to
live All the positions in dispersal

The instantaneous without
perambulation lost
cancel una sola occhiata
subsuming immediacy left in
the varieties of constipation
Tactility a rhetorical figure
without felicity of apposition
Interpenetration a kind of virus
beyond the elegance of microform
Grace and passion expended in a mass
market consistent with its death mask

Crab Walk

IN THE NATION'S UNCURTAINED SICKROOM

VARIETY OF PAVEMENT TEXTURES

RESOLVE THE RIVAL CLAIMS OF DIFFERENT TRUTHS

A WOBLY

PRETENTIOUS STUMBLE

CHANGING THE ARRANGEMENT IN STIMULATION

CHANGE THE STIMULATED TO PATTERNS BACKED UP

BY OBSERVATION

EMPTY RESONANCE OF A NUMBER OF COVERED PASSAGE-WAYS

TO ENTERTAIN THE UNKNOWN GOOD IT HOVERED THERE

A SUFFICIENT NUMBER OF PROCESSING UNITS COUPLED

WITH EFFICIENT TRANSFERRING

THAT WHICH MOST I WONDER AT   STOOD AT THE GATE TO BE PLEASED

SUDDEN TEMPERATURE DROPS

WITH SPEED

TAKEN UP WITH JOY

THE AURAL SHOCK OF EMERGING INTO A HIGH STREET

TOGETHER WITH THE RISE IN SEA LEVEL

TRANSFERENCE AND CERTAIN RANDOM

MY SENSES WERE INFORMERS TO MY HEART

BEHAVIOURS

FRACTAL STRUCTURES CULMINATED IN A DENSE FRONT

AS IF MT TREASURE AND MY WEALTH LAY THERE

WIDER THAN THE SKY

weed spawn water staircase
white walss Itten yellow tips
then bullfinches possibly pink
earth blue sky petrol green
cheap tricks in the metal case

speed wrn sandstone
flight sails bitten
chirps against
fettles race

stealth with Grace he has survived
an inner fight to sit down and apply paint
lifts you out of the cage forged from your memory
your emptiness Unafraid to be afraid just because
it's getting warm here Arrhenius just because this
rubble will take a million before our swank names it cool

Balance achieved
a dynamic arrangement of shapes
weight and volume pulling in different directions
a feeling akin to exhiliaration caused by the poise's repeated
sense of reassurance even relief from the recognition
that all the elements combine the resolutions
of potential conflict within
peace and serenity
plastic emotion
the beautiful

collimate

collimation includes the process of aligning various parts of
an optical light system where matter is dynamically
negligible near the singularity

I made a collimator using old toilet roll centres some blue-tac
and a couple of razor blades involving limiting a beam of
radiation to required dimensions

a fine slit at the principal focus of the convex lens in a
spectroscope operates as a prism separates the colours reveals
a complex of bright and dark lines labels the condition of the
light's source

Curie

At night workroom bottles of liquids and capsules of crystals
eyes accustom to dark see feebly luminous silhouettes of
containers glowing

Stood and watched "stirred with ever new emotion and
enchantment"
At a seance table their hands raw and burnt from radium

the medium between two physicists her right foot on one of the
physicist's left foot her left on the other's right

a disembodied spirit manifested 'fluid emanation'
'ectoplasmic materialisation'

the light suddenly switched
the medium naked of her weighted shoes
waving butter muslin

depressed and permanently tired
ideas on the culture dreamed of dispelled
disenchanted with radioactivity

dance

her right foot on one of the physicist's left foot her left on the other's
right

a completely civilised art
remarkable lucidity
the body clear to eye the feet distinct from the legs the legs from the
trunk the shoulder the arms the head each separately defined

danced while I hummed to fit rhythmic patterns to them with my feet

news flashed laboratory to laboratory parity not conserved
remarkable lucidity afoot
the physicist broke away from a food queue danced a jig

disk

A man in an orange flying-suit crossed an arena carrying a large disk of clear acrylic with perpendicular sides. Polarised light projected through the material made clear that the perfect shape of the form was made possible by extreme tensions. A completely civilised art. On the screen an action replay, a multi-coloured moiré pattern. Dropping the disk into nitrogen and projecting the light again showed the disk freed of tensions, but misshapen.

As a globular cluster plunges through the strong gravitational field of our galaxy disk it produces a wake in the disk's star distribution. This wake involves a density enhancement behind the cluster, which creates a gravitational drag, a tidal friction, on the cluster's motion. A disk allows a higher ratio of surface area to volume than a sphere indicating a maximum rate of exchange with the environment.

When a drop of blood is examined microscopically it's easy to distinguish the types of cell in the plasma. In humans the most obvious are the red disk-shaped blood cells slightly concave on both sides. Astronauts in zero gravity develop 'spikes' on their red blood cells during their time in "space". The phenomena of the spiked disk has been prohibited by the death of red blood cells after 120 days.

duck-pillow

on the screen an action replay a multi-coloured moiré pattern.

the screen a multi-coloured moiré pattern on an action replay

on the moiré pattern screen a multi-coloured action replay

the screen pattern a multi-coloured moiré action

on the pattern a coloured moiré replay

a moiré replay on the coloured pattern

multi-coloured moiré action on the screen pattern

a moiré action replay on the multi-coloured pattern screen

a multi-coloured pattern action replay on the moiré screen

a moiré screen action on the multi-coloured replay pattern

Dog

"sum of respective average values equal to 8
after appropriate corrections for the periphery have been made"

In fog came women, children inhumed in stone cists, hides simple things
from north-west Greece, Epirus, Albania, with flowers, perhaps orchids
from Ukraine, and Transcaucasia, bad weather lifts
orange carton corner, north of the Pindus, burnt
in the wake of arrival, no future time will think of these
devastations, respect the land, blown leaves shift wrought stone
came from any ages styles, dance, you don't tell others to
override one another in struck fashion, sung forever

To northern mists, inhuman bone wrists, find gratitude
wither hours, sad wetter rifts, mauve darkens fauna
waste pits rejects out of hand, brought home in phases
piles applied smother, luck fast Kleptovariants, bold randy,
what to you ran amuck, clenched foster, loathing rides off Desire
found outside phrenetic roll, now rain now wonder in vein
reserve bust meant an economic computation theory climax on statics
seeing through signs felt risk spurt nodes of sex change

Men, Women, Barbarians, Badgers
old angry with cities, not truly animal drenched
posture, clothing and ideas of Beauty ground
without direct genetic control, no pain no understanding of pain
serves adjustment to ecological community
the recent climatic fix on their movement
meaning new economy, self-sufficiency
subverted by modes of exchange, by copulation

During the most recent warmer times sprung as we draw near
they moved north from the warrings with honey with honey bee
mountain Hares and heath butterflies over solitude
with Beaver folk in wooded parklands on its surface
maybe 3 or 4 hundred of them, made oracles from bone from ashes
joined a forest culture using fish-hooks flints dug-out canoes
broad-bladed paddles, played the races, watched the burnings crack
layers of blue blue-grey throat-cleared sounds of frolic laughter

Pleistocene as if the soul rung with as much proximity
grooved forth beneath wearing hoar frost doubt in shales and
shade pollinates solipsistic weavers stood naked in a surfeit made bundle
frayed futures loaned and cashed coined restatements
from Gilgamesh cut into Mississippi Delta flood the yearnings back late
bird song slate balls resounds melancholia let to bait or lot of fun
avoided deep voice marked baulk at soak render Shiva greetings multiple
hand grasp in the brain bowl's wrought image

Words divided beyond equal portion into jet stream drained sumps set car
skin before the rot mashes another by-pass solo over violin network. More
recently that has led to boar and aurochs, loss and flutter, hedgehog and
red-throated diver on market boards, men and women folk bend call
Beavers, congregate in large furs handing crisp exchange for slivers of red
deer held in store against shortage. In Worcester provided Beverage in
Beverstone served pie named Broad-Tails, fetched 120 pence for their pelts
against 12 for trims of otter robe, crash 30 cars to pieces on summer time

Broad-Tails last seen on strong banks of the Tivy
construct castles mid river receive on their bellies logs of wood
cut by associates feet held thus transverse placed in mouth drawn
backwards fasten'd with teeth to raft entwined willow
different leaves with four teeth nothing else here
they haven't been around since colliers took the trees precise
out since the worst users of energy, the speculators unstrung
started intransitive verbs hard skin strong shoulders

I met the blue Hares of the north often sunlight
about this time moulting into full white pelage against grey hills
long silky belly hairs brush snow as they skitter
frozen moors avoid plains or beaten paths
but use woods avoiding city dogs
where rankness of herbage doesn't check their speed their sadness
These Puss, we named them, the most merveylous shut out
believed to be hermaphrodite rise out their forms

to pasture or return to their seats one way dark waves
in order not to suffer twig or grass to touch but
would sooner break it with teeth to make way
and in chase will make cross roads ten or without need
twelve times will make their ruses their false paths
I sometimes meet a solitary Hare in the open or in a 'form'
a tuft or grass selected to give a good field of view shouting
shelter from some prevailing wind the tidal

It was as if she'd just been born new pillows rest on you
fully furred with eyes ears open and smouldering
carried by doe to separate forms and suckled
In her exposed habitat defenceless against
fox stoat polecat feral cat words lost in gasps
When mature this problem goes Hare's large side of head eyes
wide-angled vision improved by sitting hind legs
Like Deer difficulty detecting stationary objects clenched erases us

will lope leisurely up a path quiet
to within feet of a whiteman standing motionless sparkling
Buck with buck in season will box or skip on hind legs refuge
rapidly vigorously forefeet leap into air at each other's bellies
Concentrated on airfields attracted by noise or vibrations rosy armed
of aircraft as they are by thunder the radiation emitted by power
lines and information terminals I've met herds of 400 fruit
in such places before the dogs came before the cities' lairs

[209]

On a November day in Perthshire 6 guns shot 1289 hares
Extraordinary lengths are gone to block this lucidity
They're as often killed by mowing and reaping machines fatigue and
      straw
toxic alkaloid cystisine and sparteine bark of broom
but immune from myxomatosis you stand before the silver
Some night you'll hear Badger-cries lack people
Peace good soul shortly death dropping waters
My grey pale lifts from its sett in a cromlech fragrance

to travel to circles or brakes in cairns loud-moaning
To fight extermination using deer park refuge from hunter
accused of stealing chickens and eggs strange golden clouds
instead consume large quantities of insects lakes
sometimes rats mice voles rabbits earth worms acorns
more often fish and organic sweet corn gentle gaiety
I sometimes sleep 60 yards in from white-armed contrivance
rest entrance   Using derelict waste lovely tresses

my ramifications can be three storeys necklaces
of tunnels over an acre of woodland fleet of foot
ideally deciduous with ample ground cover
of furze broom shrub but including abandoned mine shafts sitting
      opposite
Three of my dogs are lurchers licked
the cross-bred grey-hounds spring smoke light
that Gypsies use to catch food heard all this
Although their coats are rough finishing all distance

they are gentle, prissy creatures hold my hand
with a horror of muddy feet among the deathless
and an aversion to rough games. the lyre and wobble box
My residence in Britain goes back to hedgerows herdsmen
just after the dawn of consciousness. turns slowly
The place names of pate and bawson wide pathed

brock and grey are added to the palette after red and blue
Or Badger ham on the menu produces a violet hue

Older than and tangled by cities amazed all laden
they haven't been there since collars were invented
in such places before the dogs came with woodland
just after the dawn of consciousness a golden flower
I came west through the ice a silver bow
from perhaps North Africa inhabiting sands and uplands turned dark
in my wake the norm of devastation civilised

The map of this place no longer matches its present form
under ice-sheets and glaciers wild hyacinths
preceded by stone tool-makers makers of chipped flints
I knew nothing about their hand prints their children
imagery their teeth imaging
marks their fire tools their graces their gazing
I can only tell you they searching
could count and I'm told sung strain of past days

spoke about their lives as animals stand on
I came west through the ice necklaces
smashed the ice came concealed in a mammoth
the drama walls the fire signs or
drum beats last we heard north of 1910
in fact human tools in coupling with
a consequence of natural force tongues and clutter
known as Palaeolithic drenched light

An age a thousand times longer than since the Great Flood alone
Contacts with these Ancients gets confined to their stone tools desire
incorporated in geological deposits silt and sound
and occasional rare skeletal remains before cave dwelling
The two tool shaping methods set in with Pleistoceners after the bad ice
either using the Asian idea of flint nodules chipped until a double-faced

core emerges or the African method of striking off a substantial flake
working that single face into implement enviable in mien

The Euro-ancients overlap methods that shape us
The core toolers became known as Acheulian daybreak
Britain, as well as Europe, Africa, Palestine and most of India silliness
        and sorrow
the Swanscombe consciousness contemplates piles of mollusc shells
on Thameside contemporary with Abbevillian the Cromer flake culture
leading to the Clactonian techno-complex and hand-axes
A thousand distinct molluscs within a mile of here
a solo thrush taking each snail one at a time to smash their shells

The blade tool hunters follow carving bone gleaming feet
multi-barbed harpoons spears thus lever moods
and flint against metallic rock fire making 20,000 years ago impatient
animal paintings engravings caves murmur quiver
in Derbyshire, Wales, the Wye valley, the Mendips
Aurignacians included skilled hunter artists
technicians of flint trim followed the gold tressed
by Gravettians from south Russia and elsewhere

the first specifically British culture whirrs
counterpart to French Magdalenian shredded
already varied racial characteristics in remains
Most of late Palaeolithic Britons Cro-Magnon thanks
the Red Lady of Paviland South Wales yage fodder
a young man with an elephant's head under red ochre
Mesolith in Britain threefold immigrations
in the process of England's insularity around 8000 years ago

and damp oak woods with abundant alders replaced pines iconostasis
Forest culture of Maglemosian fishers and fowlers with powder
canoeing from east diet supplemented by hazel nuts luck like that
and vegetables and two neat-fingered microlithic cultures

the Tardenoisian known as the Shadows with their dogs
from perhaps North Africa inhabiting the sands and uplands
and the Azilian fishermen shell-fish collectors fowlers and hunters
were strand-loopers along the newly formed coastal fringe

Which confirms us Barbarians as landowners sincere
for more than a quarter of a million years in Britain
We excite admiration for the way we are coping rattle the empty car
with life in the twentieth century. You and I
When midnight a host of dogs and men go out
track the Badger get a forked stick chapping
bear him down clap the dogs in wave wash
take him to the town for baiting

We are perceived as Foreigners everywhere small animals
non-Christians, non-Hellenes, rude, wild
uncivilised natives of Barbary soft spoken
Cromwellians with forehead badges,
dealers in corn, insisters clash swift-footed
Irritated Egyptians name us the northerners the glorious
all lands ramshacklers, destroyers of bronze Ugarit, bronze Alalakh,
unsold shirts attackers of Mycenae and Troy hail-healers

Thirty-two centuries before the present, day-old
from Hallstatt, from La Tête, refuge from sea raids, hard of heart
around Mediterranean shores in boatloads delivered counsel
as early as thirty-six centuries past, hecatombs
burning, the Komarow pyre-graves,
burning hot-foot, orchid sunshine, scorched earth
in my wake, in my awakening, the chemical art transforming,
cities of self-cremation, fire-breath pollution,
common insecticide, the norms of devastation civilised, without
        tinkering.

Work Consciousness Commodity: Three Kinds of Perception

1. Ditty Bop Walk

The radical alternative begins in awkwardness:
Badgers' discourse of production embeds upon return;
Technics describes the tactics of living, Outward's
procedures of conflict.
Discourses of production, representations, exchange on satellite
war-economy blurs the imaginary; reproduces determinant
instances as a continuum.
Each machine *serves* one process owes existence to
thought about this process. Let me out,
Badgers say, Liberation of productive forces needs to be
confused with liberation of cities. They stand on the edges of a London
        that constitutes war-economy itself. Every Badger
knows and dreads the *emptiness* that follows labour power.
Normality purchased as a value.
In contrast to quantitative measure, use value remains a
qualitative potential. Tied in their thinking to the present,
Badgers know or smell death as something in the future that
does *not* threaten them.
The use value of labour power is the moment of its rockhouse.
This is the rockhouse the Badgers' relation to their useful
expenditure of effort.
"We're going to sack the City."
The quantitative signifies only the commensurability of all
work in terms of exhaustion; the qualitative, under the pretext
of incommensurability, goes much further. It signifies *the*
comparability of all carbon life in terms of production and
labour. The abstract and formal universality of commodity
labour power supports the "concrete" universality of
qualitative labour. There are no "humans-in-themselves" only
humans and those that resemble them. They contend in battle
with a *given* world. The universe moves on with stockbroker concern.
Mohican hair cuts proceed down backs in braids of wire.

In this structuralized play of signifiers, the fetishism of labour and productivity crystallizes. Every drop of water is a battlefield.

"We challenge the human capacity of energetic, physical, and intellectual production. The productive potential of every Badger in Western society transforms the environment into ends useful for Badgers and not for the society that burns them." Long noses sense out the coming devastation.
In the structural sense, within the totality of existence, within all that can be described, labour necessarily precedes play. The Badgers work at play as a breaking off *from* labour and a recuperation *for* labour.
Badger-play is purposefully *unproductive* and *useless*.
"We cancel the repressive and exploitative traits of labour and leisure." The higher herbivores are ruled by the ear and by *scent*. The higher carnivores *rule with the eye*.
This realm beyond London economy called play, non-work, or non-alienated labour, is defined as the journey without end.
In this sense it is a consciousness and remains
aesthetic with all the bourgeois worry which that implies. Torn jackets and jeans do not exempt this observation.
The world-picture is the environment as *commanded* by what can be described. The state of civilisation becomes continual mass extinction. From the viewpoint of social distribution and consumption of communication, labour is always a value of use or exchange. Value is measured by the quantity of time socially necessary for production. Let's not forget that *work could be apprehended outside value,* on the side of the commodity produced and circulating in the chain of communication. Here labour no longer represents any value, meaning, or signification. It is a question only of a *body* and a constellation of descriptions There is an infinite sense of power in this quiet wide-angle vision, a feeling of freedom that has its source in *superiority*, and its foundations in the knowledge of greater strength and consequent certainty of

being no one's prey. The world is the prey and the existence
of Culture has always had this dependence.
A Badger stands on the Yat in half-light watches the
picturesque sink into the mud of the Wye. Property is the
domain in which unlimited power gets exercised, the power
gained in battling, defended against peers, victoriously upheld.
"The labour of the sign", and "productive inter-textual space,"
are ambiguous metaphors, sponge cakes made into trifles;
absorbant and instantly consumable.

The fight of nature-within against nature-without is not
misery, but a grand meaning that *ennobles* life. To be
rigorous the meaning must be surpassed and annulled. It thus
becomes necessary to emancipate humankind from the
nineteenth century idea of an "evolutionary" process. I catch
trout for myself to eat, it's that obvious, ownership that simple.
Doesn't matter whether it's comprehended or proven, the cities
of world-history plummet from catastrophe to conservatism.
The remains of those before me are as old as their tools. In
addition to the "thought of the eye" the comprehending and
keen glance, humankind now has the "thought of the hand".
The question of whether something is suitable or unsuitable—
the criterion of the Deer—has nothing to do with that of true
and false, the values of the City. The Badger-soul strides
forward in an ever-increasing alienation from *all* Culture.
The fight is hopeless and fought out to the bitter end.
Piracy is as old as navigation, raiding of the trade-route as
conservative as nomadism, and wherever there is peasantry
there is enslavement to a warring nobility and economy. The
animals of the City who made others their domestics in order
to exploit them, have taken themselves captive. The great
symbol of this fact is the human *house*.

2. Dixieland One Step

Beavers seek out the period's most avant-garde texts. They're almost coy about it. This develops a complicated theory about the role of the imagination in the artist, the prelude to *another* Aesthetics. It helps the discovery of the concept of contingency and the invention of the notion of a totally secular freedom followed from the intuition of intellectual needs. Beavers live a paradox. It is their business to create what's necessary to them in that which they are unable to raise themselves to the level of. Beavers see sadness and boredom in their depths—as free as they wish but impotent. Their decoy duck is adventure; rational determinists who believe they are free. Beavers are said to be unhappier than Badgers, but far more pleasant to deal with. This is said with caution.

"For some time now you have been wondering about hope and despair."
The distinction between *to be* and *being*, and the investment of being with the relation, movement, and efficacy that had resided in existing, shifts into a discussion of building and housing. There is a distant applause followed by gun fire. The whole of this is witnessed by those in the role of "anonymous passers-by".
Beavers move for the liquidation of the acquired heritage, and the invention of a new form. Time-binding is not on the active agenda. Everything seems to spin around ideas of freedom, life and authenticity. Irrationality will not be suppressed by masking. Hair oil marks the wall of passage, the pillow case, the coat collar.
He immediately started talking off the top of his head, without notes, sitting on his desk—we had never seen anything like it.
Anger is the last resort of the weak or of the domestic mammals staggering under the weight of a full briefcase.
The City provided an unprecedented cultural success: scrimmages, blows, broken chairs, fainting spells. The doctrine which makes human life bearable. The themes are

individualism, responsibility, angst, commitment, solitude, and the notion that hope relies on action. Dried vegetables line the gutter of the Saint-Germain-des-Pres. There is a shift from matters of being into those of freedom. Beavers couple this to praxis which the English read as any meaningful or purposeful human activity, any act that is not mere random, undirected activity.

Badgers meet Beavers in confinements. The only sounds are the footsteps of guards. Daylight filters through a thick grid of fluorescence remains lit all day. Conditions of life in the City are intolerable.

The only thing that matters is the relationship between the individual and Being. But Beavers are never individuals, it would be more fitting to call them universal singulars and requires simultaneous examination from both history and what is proposed.

"As a Badger you have astonished, upset and denied all that has turned our society into what it is today. This is what I'd call the extension of one's potential. An action that gives power to your imagination. Don't give it up."

The question was not so much to bring animals together as to bring ideas together.

The Beavers discuss travel, polygamy, transparency. The counterculture based on these notions added provocation and the hatred of clichés, conventions and domestic animals. "You give me regret," and "It makes me all poetic," and "It has seldom made me so gratuitous and so necessary" become their cries of war. In front of the City they bemoan that nothing new could happen to them. They are seized by fits of nostalgia for "lives of disorder" and authenticity. Work and love take place in broad daylight, and anyone can intrude at any point. No private property, no compartmentalisation, no secrets: a social life down to its barest essentials, or almost.

[218]

The Beaver streets in pursuit of papers shaking with laughter blinded by wet eyes. Projects propel each Beaver forward. The discovery of a spectral reality, a skeletal City, the sodden awareness of chaos and war. The pride of consciousness facing the world, origin of their absolute freedom, a special relativity. A consciousness that is at once a merging and a wrenching away, a freedom that is at once a fever and a discipline, a state of permanent criticism, a mistrust of all fixed and crystallised social roles. Beavers are estuant against digestive philosophy. Hot under the collar, gagging, magically extracting, from the darkest spacetime of oppression, an appeal to freedom and individual anarchism. In a disregard for historical factors the City is said to follow the Beavers the intruders the outsiders the marginals. It is the City's sustenance its aesthetic nurture. That is the hypothesis. They meet the Badgers in a wild rush of words and juxtaposed ideas from tired bodies against time-rush and sleep-space in occasional lapses of absence from which they promptly emerge to resume attempted control. The meeting between them was not on the sofa but imagined there. Beside a series of bookshelves in the house a large desk, a bay window, they concentrate mutual critique and subsequent reliance. The becoming of the age of the public dwelling made private consciousness.

3. Double Shuffle

Wounded Stag on a high hill frond pronounced hailstones.
The self possibilities of materials and expression of the area
lived in. Thick darkness, shame and incomprehension war blast
from nostrils. In a step-like cultural change from cows and pigs
and hay and all what farmers have to do involved in art. Alert
ears, *the laughter of gods*, Miriam the Prophetess, pull together.
May 19th *Hereford Times*, burnt out cars on Royal Ordnance
Bomb Disposal fields at Wellington. "Soon we will be too late to
realise the anthropological understanding as a basis for an
alternative society of the future." "The work of those who go
out may be worth more than those who sit in the corner."
Fuzzy sets and their applications are in a reel from pleasurable
activity.
Another thud apple, blame local blackbird, or din of
earthmover builds by-pass surgery vibrations in her stomach,
cabbage white under slate of a first fruit tree.
Without inner transformation on an individual level, political
upheavals are merely power changes. The stag appears in
times of distress and danger with another understanding of
freedom, realisation of freedom in culture. To get free from
the restriction and indoctrination and ideologies of States and
economical interests in Western private capitalistic systems
and in Eastern State bureaucracies The hare remains bound
by genetic programme, remakes identical form. Give Hare a
place to stand and the earth moves. Culture, democracy and
economics
are funds of society. The Hare insists upon self-administration
rather than state monopoly or private capital. At the normal
working place a few strange additions. More emanates from
these than if the ideas behind them were merely revealed
directly. Heal like with like, but also reveal a gift to the self.
On a platform in a square from melted down gold images of
Hare and a sun, a "small, peace object" turns the cultural and
economic empathy back on itself through that normal place
with its added strangeness. "Now we speak of the invisible

sculpture, the ideas of creativity and self-determination in an alternative social situation." That is the wider understanding and only a beginning.
The problem of democratic laws stand in an organic relationship to the position of freedom.

Everybody can have a kind of dream, a kind of feeling, a kind of deeper relationship to nature, to humankind as kin, to the society, to the environment, to the future, to the soul, to the will condition. Meet together working with potatoes or with plants or with a present practice in industry that is criminality in doings in which the youth will hate so much because the reality of the social body in the field of the free spaces in the culture in the education in the information in the mass media is the destruction of the creative instead of its potential as cooperative as connectedness with all different fields as a rich cohabit of use from the existents with the imagined.

5. Fizz

Grind

Sight catches wings in clover
Compost purple
Field system
Dry river flood reeds
Swan belly swan air
Eddies ripples turbulate
Reverse river
Then turn soil then deposit
Cold face
Not sorrow nor surface
Distant posts and poles
Wind catch
Red fog detectors
Breath shapes

Parrot-head starts move in Pleistocene spring
artifacts of wood in the wake of the ice
Chest jewellery Maize Man contrasts Bat Man
used as a receptacle shaped like a lung.
An aerial view of a sacrificial meadow
maps a spacetime of dedication
unrealistic hope perpetuated by stress
Stone faces eating incense and mushrooms.
Collapse followed by settlements preceded by
civilisation, resisted dragon with inverted hair
known as Feathered Serpent
built ritual site dedicated to Flood and Rain
Parrot-head in the city carries coloured speech
sings to the music of Spring and Sowing.

This is the morning of the vulnerable male homage to
the "Flayed Lord" displays of red flesh the skin of another's slavery
Below my chest a scar where my heart was removed. Dance
with Death and Capital, female resilience in a gold breast-plate
conflicts invasion an androgynous Gold-ear listens
from a cage the first permanent settlement
An ancient painting guide to the collection of relics
gives a key to these riddles, rediscovers a lost resistance
Geographic writing, scientific letters, a history of the textiles
contrast highlit glyphs, mythology in motion, and torture on video.
Invasions and expectations, derivations and inventions
flag an end of civilisation and separates when from where.
Loose-leaf sheets settle into a plan for the city without a garden
Value translates into a loaned summer that will not exist.

Light on white mud on clover
Mushroom compass
Calendars new teatime
Dried reeds from meadow flood
Winged bulb lilies
Float pad
Against river of different flora
Flood gully winds
Old leopard space
Sorrel leaf tips above surface
Signal flood ponds
Tree bridge across Lugg flow
Crack willow and alder
Salute musk past.

Fish-Tail

Dream releases a hare
before the Civilian transforms her
Consciousness of pleasure
retarded by memory
The gravity of occurrence has
made itself felt at once
a sacramental momenergy
trapped within concoctions of another spacetime.

Usurped their own Being
and need for safety
mother, warrior, hag, virgin
alerts to
prosperity to land use
an emblem of the planet as home
protection of flocks and herds
usurped by children.

Oracles are consulted
but first constructed
In times of social danger
the usurped are wizards and
liars They are swans and ducks
they are war ravens and geese
they are corpse birds from
other worlds invented in dreams.

They are transcendent and circular
Over and above the numerous personal ornaments
and vocabularies,
elaborate parade weapons and repetition
with recurrent apotropaic designs
a wealth of wooden idols, the simulacra,

crude and direct bog figures or male figurines,
symbolic of obvious functions.

In the garb of torn ground cover
the Hunter scoffs at hints of shrines
and ritual pits, of votive wells and
sacred precincts from behind
a screen of artistic and ethical standards
traditions at once alien and incomprehensible
more than 2000 years ago
the Hunter begins to wear heavier boots.

A partial change of burial rite signals
a spread of power
an extensive network with more than one focus
linear patterning, spirals, bird shapes
in torcs, pottery, ivories and land forms
signal inspirations and migrations
from plant and foliage and
zoomorphs with winged stencils elaborate knots.

Compare mirror with mirror
others pushed east
jugs with invented limbs in handle
from grave and helmet with iron and gold
mountings lost cheek-guards knobbed finial
influx from heroic ideals of tribes
sword scabbard in ceremonial prowess
left in disuse since discoveries of iron.

Continuity of stylised horse motifs with reversed heads
on silver coin and gold stater struck at
retreat dates from defeat
Fretted enamelled plaques,
part of horse's harness with work using Champlevé

recurrence of motifs a new millennium
a dot of light bounced in and out formed a pattern
incorporated into decoration and ritual pursuit.

2.

Metal, stone and leatherwork and illuminated manuscripts
humankind chariots a new vocabulary and Being
man with foliage mouth
becomes face-urn with death hair moustache
full of written-out mythological fragments
euphemised into legend and tales
overlapping ecocatastrophes
and heroic events.

Cascade rubble and animal sounds
quieten into a float-past of clothing
interrupted by the sick thrown in rivers and
parcels of food on the water
as offerings for immaterial ancestors
feast thought of as sacred on lakeside mud beds
gives rise to new growths and wisdom
hazel shoots carried away by salmon or the mouths of
        mammals.

Foliage designs in wall painting and mosaics
Sacred trees and groves
venerated for what they stand for
column the great tree the great route of Being
felled in 1914 made dynamic
in support of cleansing war
trees fashioned into figurines timber roof supports
now in the trenches new men grow green shoots.

Cult of graves and burial rituals shrines
with sacrifices human and animal continuity
grave mounds chthonic and fertility selfish
human experience votive deposit insurance
cult origins romantic antiquarian speculations mask popularity
priesthood bogus roles of wise-men, shape-shifters,
shamans, prognosticators without social dignity
without religious connotations of their pagan know-how.

Predilection for human sacrifice
great wicker-work images filled with humankind
set on fire Cult of the head and identity
underworld and motif of severed thought
in every period and geographically widespread severed from body
after death decorated war trophy
the slain constituting
military prowess in the head carrier and banner.

Solar implied halo of burial ash suggests heads
embalmed in cedar oil enemy's distinction
preserved in chests exhibited alongside wells
recovered from underground pool between
material and presumptive portraits
hung from belt trepanned trophies
independent after death cup in crown as font
phallic on stone pillars as life-force

Horned birds hover antlered form
both bovine and human ears wears torc
over antlers or holds it wears long garment
on one plate cross-legged tailor's seat
holds great ram-headed serpent
keeper of the treasure concerned with wealth
and what issues from fertility prosperity
commerce death to art and empire.

[230]

A serpent vomiting money
from subterranean stores
emerges from basaltic floor where
wealth has mineral form
Guardians inside barrows
protect warriors of the scientific fortress
horned helmets warrior king as healer
holds caduceus in left the keeper of medicine

3.

Bright, shining in river names
clear water as place of polis, city
absorbs and reflects sky's fire lake
energetic intelligence the consort of breath
husband to clearing land for pasture
creative freedom, healer and survivor
dreams the antlered dancer pulls a golden thread and spins
to protect humankind without need for martial success.

Frug

Coverage in language literature of art, design and culture continues to be discussion encompassed by continuously coming across the invasions which mark the northern limit. Influence can be experienced indirectly through the work of other peoples. Many of the towns and cities reached their prominent positions because of rule, law and commerce, particularly the seat of the imperial procurator which becomes the seat of the speculator in bronze age settlements. Legendary arrivals are put into poetry. Iron age huts and burials phase with Oriental influences. Terracotta slabs, the Bulls in Ambush, the Augurs, the Lionesses, and the Temples of severe style include the Tombs of the Monkey; the Leopards; and the Funeral Couch. The date and place changes but last peaked around London 1980-1990. The Temple of Concord's silver libation dish completes another city wall and frees states of occupation, invades, advances into valley and conquers central Deer Hunt in the Battle painting now lost but copied into mosaic floor at House of the Aversion of the captured. 2000 bronzes taken as plunder results in changing coinage from copper to silver period included the Tomb of Shields. The century of Banquets and later chamber Tombs housed the leader of planning with a swimming pool and massage unit in the centre of what was once an empire. Wall paintings include 2 views and extend to include paintings at the House of Griffins known as the Second or Repressed style. The Infancy of the Hunt frescoes and Invasion of the official gazette into senate signify male armouring. Paintings of a youngster reading from a scroll assisted by a Priestess Seated at a Table assisted by helpers while playing a lyre leads to The flagellation Dancer and Domina, The terror-stricken woman known as the wind nymph. Villa of the Dining room and Restored Bedroom aligned with Villa that enforces new calendar from March 1st to January 1st, 365.1/4 days of political change. Murder wins power with fights and suicide receives name and reorganises state, rebuilds Frieze with legends of reconstruction. Wall painting of garden, book on Architecture from Paintings known as the "Third style". Wall at House Portrait of a Young Woman with Marriage contract, on wheeled shell Drawn by Bulls panel at House of the Dining room frieze and a wall

Temple of the Avenger and Iron Sword of Honour, wood scabbard, iron blade & gold decoration restored. Death of Temple re-built Conquest of Portrait head marble, Palace with mosaics and garden now in Museum. On stair-wall dynamic, illusionistic style in art known as "Fourth style" or the style of the imagination dead. A Law Student and his Wife with Marriage contract, The Three Graces, and Maiden Gathering Flowers. House of Still Life with Bird, Peaches and Glass Jar Painting, are evidence of a new pattern of connectedness—a new consciousness. The Fountain of the Serpent, Earthquake destroys many buildings, a large part burns down, are part of an overlap with the past which dominates all human culture. .Bronze Lamp decorated with a Mouse Serving table. Fresco in Tomb Sign for Public Snack Bar. Eruption destroys some of this lively message, but author of source for art history prefers "Factual Classicism" in art. The Interpretation of Dreams. Mosaics after earthquake and repairs. Romantic Classicist art, art of the period of cemetery portraits on wood tied over mummies. The period specified as spanning the first four centuries of the era. Portrait of a Man relates a dichotomy between beautiful human form and naturalistic style. A corpus of pamphlets in vernacular emerges as basis of earliest mythological sarcophagi in workshops. Oval sarcophagus in "Excited style". Art including mythological, battle, and marriage sarcophagi. Leaping Buck, Tomb of Equestrian statue of same period as invasion of northern Helmet, plates shaped & riveted together reliefs. Guide describes art treasures seen by artists and patrons. Silver Bowl with handles, Bronze used for frying eggs or baking cakes. Earrings from writer of 2 books with descriptions of pictures supposed to be in a collection. Grandson added a third book. Breakdown of classical art. "Pointillistic" and "woodcut" styles in sculpture, same period as invasion. Development of centre of learning replaced by a Hall of Fame. Late Empire Tetrarchic expressionism in art. Sea Monsters Mosaic, Captured Bison. Mosaics in Villa of Women. Mosaic statues legalised by Arch. Late Antique re-integration of form, "Abstract" style and surface classicism. The Hunting mosaic at sarcophagi frieze. Palace and Basilica. Day for the Birth of worship reinstates destruction of pagan temples all over empire, building on top of them. Refined, Abstract, Patterned classicism, Silver Spoons, Pewter Flagon. Mercenaries under sack plunder of treasures and art. Gradual transition to early style in glass medallion inscribed "Survival of Sculptural Workshops". In mosaic workshops Fall and Rise of power, Culmination of old economic systems. Book Cover from Reliquary, Fragments of Capture, end of Empire, Beginning of era of virtual splendour and architecture.

Eagle Rock

1.

The number
was very great and
multiplied greatly.
Texts
supply the names
over five hundred mentioned
to these be added the names
which in various Books
the number
who were recognised
was about twelve hundred.

Modern scientific study
may be said to have begun with the publication
of the accounts.

2.

The distinction between the
invaded
and settling there, built up the great civilisation.

The chief object
was self-preservation, and self-interest
with a view to material benefits
self-conceit and the laziness coming from self-conceit
Beliefs beyond the grave
placed offerings of food
in the graves of the dead

To prevent their return for food, the heads
severed from their bodies and their feet cut off
thus the living made themselves
secure in the possession of their homes.

3.

Remembrance Day in the loop
You shall send oblivion's poppies
as a funeral gift to Orpheus
dim with inanition,
I breathe the trumpet flowers,
indigo petal drift
My soul you are all in a muddle
Old grieves shall be forgotten
for the air is cool and still,
and the hills are high,
and stretch away

Pass out of one mode of existence
into another.

4.

The earliest forms
and unknown creative power
responsible for the creation of the Earth and all that is in it
represented as a man
with a frog's head, as a man with the head of a cobra,
as an ape, as a lion

The moral system and that of the new
so similar
they transferred their allegiance
in the apocryphal literature
which followed
several of the legends

The myth founded less than 3000 years ago
on the death of the Mother.

[236]

5.

In one of the Elegies
to the Spanish Republic
a configuration held in space
suddenly
recedes
into the weight
of the material.

The Fire Lake in the air
anticipates intensification
Ivory black against
reeks of
burnt bones
are companions of the flame
born of death.

Ferneyhough

The parameters of selection eventually loop
a phase shift a layout arrangement
even where it gives sensations
an intuitive composition
produced through memory and perception
the stucturalist concept of transformation

A silk-screened still-life
with crushed video tape
and feathers
provides a digitally engineered response
from both sides of the brain
produces a newly starched outrage

There's no comfort in wholeness
and even less in its recurrence.

Funky Broadway

PATTERN
Selection
mathematically
technical
Textiles
translated
Knotwork,
Patterns
Designs
Patterns
Analytical and Cosmological
Stencils,
Colour
World of Senses
Order
Design in Nature
Floral Fabrics
Colour Book
Design & Form
Grammar
Nature
art
motion
Symmetry Proportion
Art
Novelty
Colour Book
Visual Awareness
Structure in Nature
Strategy for Design
Patterns of the Ancient
Looking
Seeing
Pattern & Shape
The Development of Shape

Shapes
Paintings
Growth
Form
Abstract
Forms & Patterns
Nature
Pattern & Texture
Designs
Colour Book
PATTERN
source
concepts
mathematical
technical
Memory
Visual Memory
Mind
Nature
pattern which connects]
Ecology
CHAOS
SURFACES
Signatures
Crystallography
Form, Chance, and Dimension
Perception in Nature
Play Dice
Mathematics
Chaos
Structural Stability
Morphogenesis
Thought
Stabilization
Complex

chreod
Brain
Significance of Pattern
A Study
in Doubt and Certainty
Reflections on the Brain
the Study of acids
Organisation and Consciousness
Catastrophe
Nature
imagery and information
organization in the striate cortex

Fox Trot

1.

A preference in the culture
and aesthetics to use dance
actually and figuratively
on cave walls
and in sculpture dancer and sign
of energy as cosmic forces
becomes a familiar
transformed into animal fertility
yogi-seated and horned
on seals
the figure of intoxication
sexual pleasure and connection
to the "other" world
ideogramic broken from the oracle
self-knower and self-hangman
in the form echoes
"Who am I" and "Who is the self"
the evolution and dissolution of the cosmos.

2.

Another tendency
is to think of femininity
as the seat of the intellect
linked to the idea of the male as passive.
a theory of emotions coupled
to philosophical thought
described through figurative, coded gestures
in dancers and sculpture.
this discussion of origins,
embraces
finitude and infinity
The day to day

life, philosophical and ethical
order and the nature of human existence
To bring aggressors to oneself
rather than to encouragement passivity.
In this sense
the female heroic.

3.

"Who am I" is thought of as enlightenment.
to overcome and realise self.
by visualising the future flavours or moods
or emotions, to produce an "ocean of feeling"
interest in movement light and shade
and turned heads a transition
the moving viewer circumnavigating
many viewpoints a patchwork method
using many quotations
towards an uneven blend of statements
what is occurring a flinging outwards of
episodes and sequences
identifies human activity
recognises
an aspect of philosophy is
a discussion about the cosmos
linked with a visit to
a separate occasion.

Freeze

Paradise gardens in ceramics
Gardens eventually hanging gardens identical with Modern
    from north garden
In captivity write many books based on word-of-mouth tradition
Formal gardens ornamental pool
Alabaster figures
Gardens embassy
Gardens pharmacology
Gardens and House
Cultivation of music, dancing, chess, hunting, gardens
Wall painting
Art in a ground plan for later buildings
Forced out marches with army
Country mansion becomes armed city
Lion-like patterns in brocades
Fight invasion move of centre on caravan routes
Gardens at Palace of Eternity
Outside
University founded, translates classics, herbals & books on
    medicine
Gardens before palace
Lustre jar and earthenware bowl with cream slip
Tower architecture
Earthenware jar with turquoise glaze
School of herbs & cures, astronomy and mechanics, alchemy and
    mathematics occupy poet
Synthesis and writing
Note garden imagery
Ewer
Readings of scientific, medical, and alchemical literature
Begins to dictate "Travel" memoirs
Turquoise-enamel painted frieze tile
Turquoise glazed, carved tile, lustre painted tile
Starts wall and panel paintings
Palace and garden

Dish; arabesque carpet
Prayer Rug, fragment of carpet
Painters begin school
Garden carpet, prayer rug

Goose Neck

1.

The present begins from a break
signified for thoughtful contemporaries
this glorious sunrise
the last stage in History
world, our own time, summarised as the beginning
labelled the period of overlap with birth of the new
spacetimes that precede the phenomenological Modernists
and their traditionalist contemporaries,
look back to the "Ancients"
revered sculpture and architecture
"Bronze Age" pleasure and illuminated traits of the era
the radical and innovative performance in production.
relief to contemporaries
interweaves classicism with romanticism
like a preference for the holistic, the hierophantic, and
         mythologic
as well as a concern for the organic relationships between
         humankind and the idea of Nature in accord.
With some contemporaries, a strong regard for politically and
         socially revolutionary ideals
characterised as passionate and republican at the same time
almost uniquely informed by the world of science and industry
Acquaintance with contemporary physics and chemistry
concern for the rights and wrongs of "progress"
evident in both visual and written works
the age that redefines the Sublime
standing in awe before the blast furnace and steam hammer
the age that lifts the worldwide war machine
to an economic plateau from which it was never to descend.

2.

The progress of poetry and opening
converted into reflections on painting and sculpture
masculine ideal of beauty embodied by statuary
using drawing as a centre
derives from reassembly.
A philosopher gives that lecture on the Sun
sees a vision in a tree
attends drawing classes, collects sculpture
following the excavations enters the action
manifest imagination
in human form
machine
an experiment circumnavigation.
writing poetry
discovers electrical nature of nervous impulse.
first spinning the human soul
a philosophical essay on slavery
the sorrows of a new system, or
analysis of Ancient Mythology as history
discovers acids.
The Apotheosis of Bacchus
Large paintings in the Great Room
various scientific texts
work on electricity & the human body
borne along by the mob
arrested and released
Practical geometry nightmare in a fire balloon.
satire on a literary circle of lily-livered Londoners.

3.

Internal lighting begins.
method of knowledge is experiment
Laws of the Planetary System.
Year of the Revolution
idea of necessary contraries
main argument calls for abundance and multiplicity against
restriction, division, conflict
illustrations to Paradise
Venus rising from the sea is a hieroglyph of the republic
Year of the Massacres
The Gates of Paradise completed, scoffed at
lover of liberty climbing towards waning moon
declaration of war against the Universe
a Creationist's Inquisition begins again
commission to illustrate On the Aesthetic Education of Man
from mere naturalness to state of fulfilling sexual love
slavery as whatever prevents human visionary potentiality
society which lives by chaotic and hypocritical systems
Dreams of life
Lectures on painting
Illustrations of atomic theory
Triumphs of Temper
Working on projected city
the unity of the intellect and the senses
microscope & telescope
ratio of spectator's organs
pattern of human perception
they became the will to change.

4.

A selective map of creative work and its context
extensive use of sources predating the period
this poetry and philosophy of poetry
an extensive use of alchemical texts
sources on the strength of conjectures
songs set to music
with as much substance as
contemporary popular melodies
the paintings and engravings of the tradition
which interacts this combination of counterfeit and
        reproduction
work read by poets and visual work admired as diverse
the alienation of the Modernist condition
in the first phase of post-modernism
after 1950 and before 1968
re-seen for the clarity of those decades
as a consequence of this re-seeing
now available in popular facsimile editions
for an age of cohesive wonder and struggle
that previous generations had limited to sketches and songs.
Restored to the origin of building, or the plagiarism
of the detected designs
carved with scenes from Adam & Eve
A philosophical enquiry into ideas of Paradise
the place that redefines the Sublime
sitting in awe before the television and laser gun
the place that lifts the whole epoch's geography
and now its speed
to an economic era in which it is always late.

5.

Destroyed in proportion as their Poetry, Painting & Music, are
    Destroyed
tears up title page declares war
History of Philosophy
historical development of consciousness
as decisive in the nascent system
the Phenomenology of Mind.
the Spiritual Form begins illustrations to Book
painted in anonymous style
Arts & Sciences against kitsch
Destruction of Bad Government
Allegory Formed by imagination
surrounded by
inspiration aggregates
destroy post-industrial machines.
Tombs of Ancient Heroes
seizing the daggers
engraves outlines of pattern-book
commanding the Sun to stand still
raves about Innocence and Experience
revises Paradise
electromagnetic rotation.
not a Poet but a Philosopher
non-Euclidean geometry
not a Philosopher but a Poet
in dissenters' burial ground.
Death text produces first photograph on a metal plate.
Coming from the gleaning field the waterfalls.

Heebie Jeebies

Propellers of light
Direct air space
Seasonal hay harvest
Whistle through leaves
White air rapids
Skeletons skimming surface tension
Newly meandered
Red sand clay
Lignum strength
Sword swallows
Wagtails one saw kingfisher
A disused mill
Sounds of car rush
Occasional silence

I came as an owl to the shoulder of Northwest and established
     culture
My fellow wanderers Southwest grew small-eared corn,
squash and pumpkin.
became basketmakers in pit houses, made black & white ceramics,
     petroglyphs and decorated meal bins.
Dissipation begins in severe drought recounted in freehand murals
Invaders bring a spatter technique that shifts consciousness
displayed in weaving.
This plunder horse-mounted nomadism introduced by white Europe
stages our battle
Red in flannel introduced by white Europe
contrasts the owl's imported indigo dye
Twenty volumes of text and twenty portfolios of photography show
     our survival surrounded by reservations
surrounded by a population of white death.

Our rocks exhibit The Sacred Pipe Account of reprinted
    mythology revised by The Teachings of A Way of
    Knowledge
includes a Review of evidence of beginnings of humankind.
Our fathers produced Male Sandpaintings as a Guide to the
    Pleistocene,
the Weaving Techniques of the Sacred.
Our poetries revised the Teachings from the Earth Philosophy.
The Story of How a Story Was Made linked to drawings and
    colours
Our mothers produced Blankets, Pottery, Basketry, Beadwork,
    Masks, Amulets, Wood Carving and Ceremonial Dress.
Their story not coded red white and blue describes another
    culture.
describes unreasonable effectiveness
Her patterns are instruments of perception
and require a special conception of simplicity. This becomes a
    story of holes, knots and connectedness in a spacetime of
    now.

Disturbs the eye
Then orientation
A row of stones
Wind sound in cell rows
Takes flight
Or in suspension
An inverted canon
Tropologic grace
Excitement from underneath
When the roots tap
A coded message
In distress
Mineral waste
Recolours the dawn.

Hitchhike

The green Beaver lifts over on hind legs
takes account of a vanished dream
Instead of a variety of truth
gets subsumed by beauty
Shrouded in a duffel coat in
gangrene in photographic film
remodelled sentences the shapes of existence.

Float into rest some peripheral debate
glances every event that refuses
engagement Speculation in favour
of rejection arriving early whenever
catching a train from happiness
to poverty Stop short of the function
of creative writing short of the
decision to be an artist decrying
the push into plot turns memory.

The Self Beavers the Subject rumbling
Function modified built on debris
Watch horizon instead of plenitude
instead of stride into the sea
A crazy moment describes strategic
civility evidence of replenishing
Rows of questions in a plan chest
ordered into capital and sprayed
with poison.

Beaver being stands on hind legs
lifts over a green hill takes
account of internal morphology in view
of a vanished horizon a kind of vertigo
Instead of a discourse of truth precipitation
in a variety of solutions where beauty
gets subsumed by relationships.

Different versions of this float into consciousness
and some rest there in debate or more
often peripheral glances against backgrounds
of disappearance of every event. Plurality
at its most pungent. The new age that
refuses a politics of learnéd ignorance which
characterised engagement. 1950–1955
Renouncement of philosophical speculation
in favour of activity. Rejection of transcendence.

Beavers refer all thought and all truth to
consciousness, to the Self, to the Subject.
In the rumbling all Beavers stand their ground
their dams and river holes. Function is
ceaselessly modified. Mud flux. A foundation
built on mobile debris. Civilisation impending.
Watch this space. Horizon imminent.

But does it end transcendence?
confront an irreducible residue?
What cannot be clearly said
in this subjugation this Self referral
consciousness this Subject ha!
this rumbling. This deceit
ceaselessly qualified, pungent and
mobile in a ricochet—
an implicit system of limits and
thus exclusions knowings and
implicit unconsciousness or is it
simply a set of rules bent or bust
as received truves move towards participation
The particulate and multifaceted displacement
of moral reflection.

The focus on language isn't it the focal
what's it balanced on the reappraisal of
participation as cogent—the lie of
the moment—the supposition a point
without philosophical existence—well
then—except to say dancing—the Beavers
in bed—café life on the river side
various digressions, escapes, water chutes
transforming fear into laughter, sneer
into speech.

How to observe ideas, as possible perception
The description of phenomena the science of it
shredded into a history of truths and how
Beavers think they establish them. The elaboration
of the Self by the Self transforming through a
constant care for truth
The endless labour of that
led to useful truths, morality
as the yardstick shifts the
mortality its transcendence.

But does it end an irreducible
residue. What cannot be
subjugation this Subject
this qualified ricochet—
an implicit exclusion or
is it bent truths and
multifaceted reflection
Stopped short to question
his notebooks in a great
muddle marked at random
astonished, ping-pong joined
with picnics and the work
on destructive philosophy

[255]

on distinctions of sequence
and discontinuity.

The focus on balanced reappraisal
the lie of existence except to say
café fiction, various escapes
transforming into speech.
An anecdote of an entire era
tracked into truth about the world
and living, trapping and printing
in snow fields changing ice
shields in the snow.

How to shred ideas of how
Beavers establish the self
through constant truths and
shifts in the ice buck
the mineral resource
Another spring energy against
police treatment of squatters
in fatigue control in
emotional dependence and the
put on face against eco-misfortune.

Horse

For sometime the Architect was unprepared for understanding
and then it came to her quickly
so much so that she had expected but had never seen
what became so obvious.

Not rich enough to buy cheap things
When she was present at a climb backwards
a nascent romanticism and mature classicism in complexity
new actors scavenge the past for ancestors.

Zoned into separate conditions
Necessity continues its vagueness a projected
sublime reason from direct and negative presentation
releases suspended values.

What she does and loses
In the interest of the beautiful
reason can be achieved by indirectly presented reflection
a positive relief from anxiety.

She gets too much of what she wants much too late
When you know how to find your bearings Art becomes a
            secondary
and positive presentation of reason that insists on the
            individual
the creative wonder stooge as the source of value

A response for the quality of life and physical survival
and a resonance that offers, that demands stocks fall and rise
in generalities in requirements for judgements
to be in conspicuous subsumption

The creative activity a contrivance to appear burning
Van Gogh as Prometheus in a death culture
involved in imaginative acts of judgement
expressive counter-revolutionary bored.

She goes anywhere and says anything
the determination as hypostasis where
diagnosis becomes an example of reflective judgement
all she lacks is the consciousness of what she knows.

To sell vegetables without being imprisoned
oppositions that attack humanity
determined when the art is hidden
in the limitation on work and relative abundance.

Astonished at how much freedom bends
Sensitive intelligence into figure forms
expresses free and indeterminate accord between faculties
the present's ownership clarifies the future destruction.

Possessed by the keen desire to live in the future
In order to describe the hidden in the determination
becomes manifest exercised freely in reflection
leisure replaced by entertainment.

The people of the future fraud and visitations
on the road of thought on the destruction of creation
judgement becomes a faculty—irreducible and original
to coin slogans contemporary with maintained ideas.

The influence of the city felt through its distance from London
The insistence of questioning thought as travelling
aesthetic judgement's reflection legislates over itself
totality's return on the fragment.

The requirement of organisation, order and method
Simply describes "a product" "without philosophical theory"
just as senses regulate reasons
world-historical insults integrate into everyday seduction.

The requirement of reward, order and method
Everyone's familiar
your incapacity to determine your particular selves
the premises of an old critique explodes.

A penalty directed to the irrationality
No pretence to delimit pictorial specificity
her incapacity to conceive any unity of phenomena
a new way of walking signifies liberation.

Question whether these packages come together and blend
The being-product, the usefulness, the belonging to the world
understanding's concepts in accord with ideas of reason
the fear of not being understood.

Focus and explore function within the machine
Valid for town and for the fields
final natural unity known to us as diversity
events judge all that follows wanting.

The appearance of simplicity
Proper to anyone or anything whatsoever
where beauty cannot be assured in terms of utility
funds power in the self against domination.

An expression of reconciliation between work and life
The truth of the being-product
where beauty cannot be assessed in terms of internal perfection
death of the planet becomes the masterpiece.

In the grip of a wish-fulfilment
She seems too sure of what she calls internal description
where beauty cannot be determined by its relation to practical
      interest
everything that was directly lived moves into a representation.

The process of synergetic reinforcement
The truth of the useful without use
makes possible the transition from knowledge to desire
irreducible images of primordial displacement.

Multiplying advantage on advantage
The reflective judgement climbs back to generality
makes possible the transition from knowledge to desire
the self experienced as other.

As if progress were experiments above the average level
On the authority of the reflective hinge
the indeterminate unity of the faculties prepare for the most
      elevated
the alienation of the spectator to the profit of contemplated
      object.

Social relations mediated by images
The attempt to find out the only exercise worth doing
to clarify structure of the proper object of judgement
according to which the interest of the beautiful disposes us to
      the good.

For sometime she was unprepared
and then suddenly
what she had desired becomes understood
as the movement of the cosmos.

Hubble

> In celebration of the confirmation that the universe is
> expanding.

Suddenly the sleeper listened intensely
and what took so long
became unexpected what was remembered
obscured

No ditch rough but stinging nettles
Absent-minded attention
after an age of waste and decoration
view vectors revenge fought pesticide

Cloned as desperate renditions
Casually breaks vacancy a jet-propelled
climb guessed-at before inject and exhaust
legalises suspected values

Simply rested on grain couch
Without concern for pattern
guessed-at reprieve by indiscreetly rested attention
a pull driver flattens rock

It never becomes too easy
Often lost but momentarily refocused
without position certainties risked onto disparities
holds onto the carpet as it recedes from underneath

So we think the values are clear
and a resounded snap remainders in over-order
in singularities squeezed through the bottle-neck
existence learnt on assumption

The carpet cracks the static underway
A row of tasselled rails to prevent the viewer
evolved from involuntary excuses
in a chord ascending into blossom

But it's fixed
the rubber the liquids the wind
all this are measured
shackles in the bounce of oblivion

Tousle regrettables shut psyche in reason
opinion spat beneath the coving
vermin ridden
in the expanse of motorway drainage

From thought ignorant of cure
Repeats ornament what seems like always
recurrence and expectation rebound on each other
a series of soon-to-be continuously on view

Period living becomes style Tonight's theme is "desire"
Cretinous in bibulous ridden indeterminacy
arums infestation exorcised purely reprieve affection
plant life situation as unexpected attainment

Lambda DASH and FIX clone your DNA
into superior vectors surrounded by
Not I sites that facilitate easy excision
of inserts and rapid gene mapping

Glad at once to be failing in what is heard
Persistence off investing bought has marvelling
habeas-corpus grudge meant respect shuns vegetates plover shelf
mote reality's adjourn when crag is meant

[262]

Desire, applauded and excused
Chaos this scribe eradicates "the precise sphere"
rusted fences vegetate need on
pushed and wrist volts into gracious into Oedipal play eruption

Pyre vent of parade, applauded and excused
Oedipal puns lap cat
each vessel's limits auricular nerves
building which often told pattern erodes

Plenty pirouetted practicality
No offence you decide in a minute victory spread city
helpless barren and uniformity of phonemes
view play of squawking magnifies situation

FLASH non-radioactive labelling and
Detection system can achieve single
gene detection on your Southerns and Northerns
FeatherVolt to provide all your electrophoresis power needs

Hows planned implode bodily necessity
Pallid fortune expand fortify shields
vial "common view" thrown over perversity
funds power in the self gains domicile station

A quiet space
Taken on board as requirement
without loss of aesthetic function
the feel of confidence

Vectors of acceptance given in to employer's need
Root and beat rudder
wet fruit can of vested inturn often vernal per fiction
enough of thanatism runs after peace

Inner rip often this appeal meant
The sleeper rapidly becomes the dreamer and then the stag
leaves through the front of his chest
nothing imagined holds away from what it is

Products that take you
From your tissue your cells to high quality
library in the superior ZAP vector
incorporates the unique in-viva excision feature

Volt metering excitement then ecstasy
This is what I expected all the many whiles
rakes posture the trade-in fool nothing in the mire
the pelt perioded discover

Addressed where impediments dove this baggage full
Confirmed by presentation
black star of the intellect peppered post-lift-off
the playback interest of the intentions of beauty

Hand shakes the thumbs-up
A list of vitamins with good causes specified
ratify rupture over prop-up objection grudge bent
occasionally pitch of desire as functional

Suddenly he listened
and as ages passed
became freely immediate
as it happens.

Huckle Buck

A riddle, lament and difficulty in 26 stanzas

> "... Earth groans with men's dying shrieks as I shatter
> fruitful woods and forests, fell standing trees ..."
> from a translation by JOHN PORTER
> of the 10th century *The Exeter Book.*

Future sprawls to this immensely
Amber scrawls as if strong
Soak in breeches crowned dismembered
Weather lifted the crows objured

Notation derives from this and settles
Without destination left in contention
Array and raged nonsense nation
Need lost sight needed inside

Xenophobia orders daytime evening editions
Need these oval raids fallout pell-melled
Sexual rather than erotic mustard falsed
Reels rabbit into what must eschews

Wheat burnt in backyard and in porch
Imbeciles bring on ashes as if Saturn
Red carnations fill dull suits mention
Ache in the chest and forehead silage muck

Shit allows full cycle to tone the queasy
Wonder lunch spoilt by the travesty cussed
Able to learn how this burnt breeze
Theory of thermostatics is buried beneath

Aversion or inclination amounts to the same fear
Applied incendiary counts this soldier's border
Irrelevant to the biologist and poet on deck
Take-over is how they perceive this pinned presumption

Theme parks take the ecological decision out of play
Velocity peaks at mental escape clause overtly truer
Impious status meridian as the Inspector larches peruses
Eaten on the sick bay entrance path sat on bottom

Sites get rubbed and left with a weed crop mixed
Ten gilded bovines are led into the meadow and skinned
Days like this are seldom recorded silence assured
And love is their carrier mapped in their sinew's obsidian

Temporary or left to confuse the public to prevent treason
Out and lost in the rain wood with mosses behoving
Did not demand this beaten into submission bidden
Inside the field boundary to count each crop as leverage

Agreed or not this go ahead relies on fewer
Sanctions or sanctuary it is rested on plays
Event words sanctimonious slept under cover
Theme and intention bottled waiting the unscrew

Processed journey across field towards oracle pyre
Inscape jolted into burning fumes a new aristocracy
Beckons offers care of immunity to fire infection
Leads the solutions into carpet of plasticised raiment

Theory forgives this lack of belonging this way
Ontology formulates the centre bestiary impounded by
Jest a locket filled with aphorism around the neck precision
Toboggan lurches down spine to reinforce this lax rapping

Think before crossing the road even if you're a bird
Thimble the fingers and sew the document in marbling
Aged with candle grease and portrait to the self
To be the wigged ecologist in a stance named bent

Travel is the main theme the need for goods pursued
Sanity is not on the list of prerequisites from the pier
Judge and judged appear to be similar cretins
Work is ferocious but honesty simmers corruption

Thread is used to check the nerve fibres perused
Eaten and defecated in one day an account of fat
Yoghurt milk and bacteria there's no amount for verve
Therapy leads each participant into singular codes

Apple air leads Lugg devastation its immortality
Knot in back and tree chair's dismiss pity
Hurt it may be pollution becomes one of many themes
Agate left to roar from a barbed power station

Quest in support of lammas land against planned
Threat directs a delicacy to unsettle the tangle
Upset you might be here it becomes a field of urns
Throb loses rhythm into bedrock introduces new breeds

False stories invented reason surround city
Vapid structures interface each junction yields
Full substance of the inverted justifies temerity
Even encourages reward for robber creation

Thought clipped in harvest exhausted in the race
Propeller chipped in marvels of wastage a vent
Weather to undercut the rationality of presumption
Function shifted without care becomes opaque becomes dense

Animal fury this might be but this cannot greed
Through fumble sheets an honesty leaves shudder
Wind of coming storm predicts another restriction
Deals with social conditions as authority's ability to fleece

Indark the story produces the need to invent
Sheet of misjudgements wiped with an oily rag
West of the city the air takes a new vest
Effervescent imports to encourage drinkable fizz

Thug would be harsh accuracy ready to screw
Trussed and bribed into a satisfactory verity
Maintain the land the status the nectar
Irrelevant—oblivious they are not—denture

Missed the calm meadows the will to play
Thatch onto period style thatched and beamed files
Mends the demolished crashed into quiet fire
This fritillary row this mould of the lover

Avail—well let the language rule
Obligates each citizen—each subject on station
Thing against thing glottis against chest cough
That leads to the point of this that's rooty

Sober it may appear the cider runs over the cup
Theme repeats theme until tasteless until fried
Totality smart appearance over devastation cruelly lent
Ash to the funeral occasion and need to be punctual

Forehead held as if in anguish as if wizened
Angle from here says it's lying held fast
Web of designed protection orders to predicate
Aster on the front porch thanks for our stipends

Hully-Gully

Climbed through stinking iris and yew
Chance and necessity continues to sing true
or remember the result of the simple play of probabilities
desperately certain the pursuit is worth it.

A small group senses there's a treasure somewhere
Crimed you thinking I wish it would eschew
whoever wants dreamwork must mix all things
nomads-by-choice in the welfare of settled rings.

Up onto limestone sea bed balmy about plants
The principles of interaction between levels and slants
the device of split representation
a re-emphasis as part of a clearer formulation.

Far enough to get an impression that it's there
Upon a two time prone seep and army routs advance
inwardly full of images as measure
the complicated patterns of errors and pleasure.

Hellebore and liverwort
Principles of pattern formation that often work
the multiplicity of excitements and moments of respite
full-bloodied calm and hesitant rest.

They return and gather a large party
Held in store canned inner words
the prerogative of daring kept from uniting the mild and savage
relationships of errors clean transmission kept a constant
        average.

Nest of aroma sticky from excitement
Aggregation and transformation shifting each moment
suggests that what we need is patience
with marks and shapes already known well.

They get across hurdles they couldn't cross before
Best off a road brick he foam next site event
the free creation of impossible combinations
the indispensable dusts in comprehending the intermittent.

The moment of greatest intensity is within performance
Deep pools in the wisdom eye water
the conflagration of production order with new meaning
Discontinuity, bursts of noise with few repetitions.

Resources

Resources for *Brixton Fractals*

The following notes derive from a scan of the preface and twelve *Gravity as a consequence of shape* poems cross-referenced into the bibliography. The poems were made directly or indirectly relative to the first fifteen pages in William Blake's notebook, numbered by Erdman N1 to N15 (with the exclusion of those three solely attributed to drawings by Robert Blake [N3, N5 & N7]).

The Preface: Cage and Skilling.

African Boog: Martin's drawings to undermine any metrical completeness; Lotringer (in san serif face); Jakobson and Mayakovsky (in italics); Reid and Einstein (with inverted commas); Conrad, Ladzekpo, Tipper.

African Twist: Joris (in italics); *The Nation* (i) (in san serif face); Williams and *The Nation* (ii) (with inverted commas); Hofmann.

Around the World: calculations relating sub-atomic masses to; Brecht and Flaubert (in italics); Millers word list (in san serif face); MacDiarmid and Williams (with inverted commas); Crick, Dickens, Leacock, Leavis, *Protect and Survive*.

Atkins Stomp: Pound (with inverted commas); Miller's word list (in san serif face); George (in italics); *Investors Chronicle, Hansard*, Janson, Mandelbröt, Sedgwick.

Ballin' the Jack: Johnson, Link, Nutrition, *Protect and Survive*, Tankas, Waddington; a Chinese film titled *Two Sisters* (in italics).

Banda: Angry, Besharse, Beuys 1973, Einstein, Frescobaldi, Gris, Gorz, Jakobson, Jones, Messiaen, Misner, Meyers, Nicholson, Palmer, Reid.

Bel Air: Adorno, Diogenes (*Lives* and in Blunt), Eliot, Fanon, Gorz, Grinstein, Hammitzsch, Hofmann, Nietzsche, Leacock, Maritain, Misner, Moulton, Russell, Sweeney, Zeeman 1977, Zeldovich.

Birdland: Halliburton, Kristeva, Mallarmé, Reid.

Black Bottom: Mayan (with inverted commas); Beuys 1982, Char, Faye, Góngora, Klopstock, Ravel, Renders, Schwartz, Waddington, Wordsworth, Zeeman 1960.

Boogaloo: Albers, Arak, Close, Edwards, Hilton, Teper, Varèse.
Boogie Break: Garrison, Greimas, Glover, Grinstein, Hutter, Jameson,
    Knight, Kristeva, Lewis, Moulton, Onsager, Walls, Whalley,
    Zeeman 1979.
Boogie Stomp: Boublik, Calculus, Clusin, Dahlen, Keilmann, Neisser,
    Nunn, Olson, Poirier, Ritterbush, Salemme, Wilson.

Bibliography for *Brixton Fractals*:

Adorno, Theodor W (1974) 'Theses Against Occultism' and 'The Stars
    Down to Earth', in *Telos*.
Albers, Josef (1963) *Interaction of Color*, Yale.
Angry Brigade, The (1983) Bombing of the American Express
    Building, street newspaper stand announcement, London.
Arak, Anthony (1983) 'Sexual selection by male-male competition in
    natterjack toad choruses', Cambridge.
Besharse, Joseph C., and Michael Iuvone (1983) 'Circadian clock in
    Xenopus eye controlling retinal serotonin N-acetyltransferase',
    Atlanta.
Beuys, Joseph (1982) exhibition at Anthony D'Offay Gallery.
Beuys, Joseph (1973) *Some artists, for example Joseph Beuys multiples,
    drawings, videotapes*, California (including conversations).
Blake, William (1973) *The Notebooks of William Blake* (facsimile), edited
    by David V. Erdman, Oxford.
Blunt, Anthony (1966 and 1967) *The Paintings of Nicolas Poussin, A
    Critical Catalogue*, London, and *Nicholas Poussin*, London.
Boublik, J.H., with M.J. Quinn, J.A. Clements, A.C. Herington, K.N.
    Wynne, and J.W. Funder (1983) 'Coffee contains potent opiate
    receptor binding activity', *Nature*.
Brecht, Bertolt (1976) American Poems 1941–47 and Last Poems
    1953–56 in *Poems Part Three*, translations by Anderson,
    Bridgwater, Bowman, and Willett, London .
Cage, John (1982) *Themes and Variations*, New York.
The Open University (1979) *Calculus of Fields, An Introduction to Calculus*.
Char, René (1946) *Feuillets d'Hypnos*, Paris.

Close, Frank (1983) 'Chromodynamics', *Nature*.

Clusin, William T. (1983) 'Caffeine induces a transient inward current in cultured cardiac cells', *Nature*.

Conrad, Joseph (1917) *The Shadow-Line*, London.

Crick, Francis and Graeme Mitchison (1983) 'The function of dream sleep', *Nature*.

Dahlen, F.A. (1983) 'Simulation shows wobble period neither multiple nor variable', Princeton.

Dickens, Charles, *Hard Times*, quoted in Hayman.

Diogenes Laertius (1925) *Lives of Eminent Philosophers*, translation R.D. Hicks, London.

Dodson, C.T.J., and T. Poston (1977) *Tensor Geometry*, London.

Edwards, C. (1983) 'Glue balls', *Physical Review Letters*.

Einstein, Albert (1979) *Einstein, A Centenary Volume*, edited by A.P. French, London.

Eliot, T.S., *Four Quartets*, London 1944 (1974 edition). See also Gardner.

Fanon, Frantz (1965) *A Dying Colonialism*, translation Chevalier, London.

Faye, Jean Pierre (1964) *Analogues*, Paris.

Feyerabend, Paul (1975) *Against Method*, London 1975.

Flaubert, Gustave (1954) *Bouvard and Pecuchet*, Earp and Stonier translation, London.

Frescobaldi, Girolamo (1983) Organ music, BBC Radio 3: sudden mood changes; unprepared dissonances; rhythmic restlessness; jerky motifs.

Gardner, Helen (1978) *The Composition of Four Quartets*, London.

Garrison, David L., with Stephen F. Ackley and Kurt R. Burk (1983) 'A physical mechanism for establishing algal populations in frazil ice', Santa Cruz and New Hampshire.

George, Stefan, 'Der hügel wo wir wandeln'; 'Komm in den totgesagten'; and 'Wir shreiten auf und ab in reicher'.

Gibson, James J. (1979) *The Ecological Approach to Visual Perception*, Boston.

Glover, Malcolm (1984) 'Phase conjugate mirrors', Laser Division, Didcot.

Góngora, Luis de (1977) *Polyphemus and Galatea*, translation
    Cunningham, Edinburgh.

Gorz, André, (1982) *Farewell to the Working Class*, Sonenscher
    translation, London.

Greimas, A.J. (1977) 'Elements of Narrative Grammar', *Diacritics*.

Grinstein, G., and John Toner (1983) 'Abundant phase transitions',
    New York. See Moulton, etc.

Gris, Juan (1983) paintings in *The Essential Cubists* show at the Tate.

Halliburton, David (1981) *Poetic Thinking, An Approach to Heidegger*,
    Chicago: includes fragments translated from *Erläuterungen zu
    Hölderlins Dichtung*, Frankfurt 1971.

Hammitzsch, Horst (1979) *Zen in the Art of the Tea Ceremony*, translation
    Lemesurier, London.

Hansard, 30th June 1983, *Oral Answers*, Rooker, Thatcher &c.

Hayman, Ronald (1976) *F.R. Leavis, a biography*, London

Hilton, Roger (1980) *Night Letters and selected drawings*, Newlyn.

Hofmann, Hans (1968) *Search for the Real*, 1948, MIT.

Hutter, Kolumban (1983) *Theoretical Glaciology*, London.

Investors Chronicle, July 1983, account of Thatcher and Leigh-
    Pemberton at lunch before his appointment as Governor of the
    Bank of England.

Jakobson, Roman (1977) *Verbal Communications*, San Francisco:
    includes fragments from Glinka, Kirsanov and Voznesensky.

Jameson, Frederic(1981) *The Political Unconscious*, London.

Janson, H.W., and Dora Jane Janson (1977) Description of Roman wall
    painting from Villa of Livia at Primaporta in *A History of Art*,
    London.

Johnson, Diane (1978) reviews books on wildernesses, *New York Review
    of Books*.

Jones, David (1975) *Use & Sign*, Golgonooza Press.

Joris, Pierre (1983) a private letter to the author from Togo.

Keilmann, and D.B. Kell (1983) 'Non-linear systems: Coherent
    excitation in biology', Stuttgart and Aberystwyth.

Klopstock Friedrich (1811) *The Messiah* (1748–1800), translation Collyer
    and Meeke, London.

Knight, Charles A., with Arthur L. DeVries and Larry D. Oolman (1984) 'Fish antifreeze protein and the freezing and recrystallization of ice', Boulder and Illinois.

Kristeva, Julia (1980) *Desire in Language*, translation Gora, Jardine and Roudiez, New York.

Ladzekpo, C.K. (1982) interviewed by Melody Sumner and Sheila Davies, *Ear/West*.

Land, Edwin H. (1977) *The Retinex Theory of Color Vision*, San Francisco.

Leacock, Eleanor Burke (1981) *Myths of Male Dominance*, London.

Leavis, see Hayman.

Lewis, Wyndham (1981) *Enemy of the Stars* (facsimile of *Blast* 1 1914), Santa Barbara.

Link, Winston O. (1983) exhibition at The Photographers Gallery, London.

Lotringer, Sylvere (ed)(1982) *German Issue* of *semiotext(e)*, New York: work from Lotringer, Paul Virilio, Heiner Müller, Jean Baudrillard, Helke Sander, Martin Heidegger, Joseph Beuys, Michel Foucault, &c.

MacDiarmid, Hugh (1978) 'The Goal of All the Arts' in *The Complete Poems*, London.

Mallarmé, Stéphane, see Kristeva.

Mandelbröt, Benoit B. (1977) *Fractals: Form, Chance, and Dimension*, San Francisco: includes discussion of Sierpinskis work.

Maritain, Jacques (1953/54) *Creative Intuition in Art and Poetry*, London.

Martin, Kenneth (1973) *Chance and Order*, drawings by Martin, Waddington Gallery, London.

Mayakovsky, Vladimir (1970) *How are Verses Made?* Hyde translation, London.

Mayan prayer, see Varèse.

Messiaen, Olivier (1967) sleeve notes to *The Awakening of the Birds* and *Catalogue of Birds*, Neumann recording.

Meyers, Jeffrey (1980) *The Enemy, A biography of Wyndham Lewis*, London.

Miller, Richard (1974) Made in Togo, *Strange Faeces*.

Milton, John, *Paradise Lost* (1974) edited by Alastair Fowler, London.

Misner, Charles W., with Kip S. Thorne and John Archibald Wheeler (1973) *Gravitation*, San Francisco.

Moulton, D.E., with A.H. Moudden, A.H. Wilson and J.D. Axe (1983) 'Abundant phase transitions', *Physical Review Letters*.

Nation, The, 1982: (i) article by Peter H. Stone, December 25th, on re-employment of retired CIA field operatives; (ii) article by Giff Johnson, December 11th, on situation of inhabitants of Palau where the USA are siting a military base with nuclear equipment.

Neisser, Ulric (1982) 'Memory Observed: Remembering in Natural Contexts', San Francisco.

Nicholson, Ben (1983) exhibition at Kettles Yard, Cambridge.

Nietzsche, Friedrich (1961) *Thus Spake Zarathustra*, translation Hollingdale, London.

Nietzsche's Return, special issue of *semiotext(e)* 1978: work from Bataille, Cage, Deleuze, Foucault, Lyotard.

Norton, David and Lawrence Stark (1971) *Eye Movements and Visual Perception*, San Francisco.

Nunn, B.J., and D.A. Baylor (1982) 'Visual transduction in retinal rods of the monkey *Macia fascicularis*', Stanford.

Nutrition Education, National Advisory Committee on, commissioned by government and subsequently refused publication. Article in *Nature* 1983 by member of committee.

Olson, Charles and Ezra Pound, An Encounter at St. Elizabeths (1975) edited by Catherine Seelye, New York.

Onsager, Lars, with Eytan Domany and A.H. Wilson (1984) 'Special solutions of the Ising-lattice problem in 3 dimensions', Stanford.

Palmer, Samuel (1978) *A Vision Recaptured: The Complete Etchings and The Paintings for Milton and Virgil* (facsimile), Trianon.

Poirier, J.P. (1982) 'Rheology of ices: a key to the tectonics of the ice moons of Jupiter and Saturn', Paris.

Poulantzas, Nicos (1974) *Fascism and Dictatorship*, translation White, London.

Pound, Ezra (1970) *The Pisan Cantos LXXIV–LXXXIV*, 1948, New Directions.

Pound, Ezra (1978) *Speaking, Radio Speeches of World War II* : (2, 5, 111, 104 & 1), edited Leonard W. Dobb, Connecticut.

Protect and Survive, H.M.S.O. 1982.

Ravel, Maurice (1906) Jules Renards 'The Peacock', 'The Cricket', 'The Swan', 'The Kingfisher', and 'The Guinea-Fowl', used in his *Histoires naturelles*.

Reid, Constance (1970) *Hilbert*, a biography of the mathematician David Hilbert, London.

Renders, Elsie (1984) The gait of *Hipparion sp.* from fossil footprints in Laetoli, Tanzania, Utrecht.

Rhodes, Frank H.T., Gradualism (1983) 'Punctuated equilibrium and the *Origin of Species*', Cornell.

Ricoeur (1966) Paul, *Freedom and Nature: The Voluntary and the Involuntary*, translation Kohák, Northwestern.

Ritterbush, Philip C. (1983) 'Dürer and geometry: Symmetry in an enigma', *Nature*.

Rukeyser, Muriel, (1942) *Willard Gibbs*, New York.

Russell, Bertrand (1957) *History of Western Philosophy*, chapters regarding Rousseau and Voltaire, London.

Salemme, F.R. (1982) 'Cooperative motion and hydrogen exchange stability in protein beta-sheets', New Haven.

Schwartz, Jeffrey H. (1984) 'The evolutionary relationships of man and orang-utans', Pittsburgh.

Sedgwick, Peter (1982) *Psycho Politics*, London.

Skilling, John (1984) 'The maximum entropy method', Cambridge.

Sweeney, Pat (1984) interviews the makers of *Carry Greenham Home*, Beeban Kidron and Amanda Richardson, handout at Cinema Action.

Tankas in the Gulbenkian Museum, Durham.

Teper, M., and K. Einsweiler (1983) *European Physical Security Conference*, Brighton.

Thom, René (1975) *Structural Stability and Morphogenesis*, translation Fowler, Massachusetts.

Thompson, DA. W. (1961) *On Growth and Form*, Cambridge.

Tipper, J.C. (1983) 'Rates of sedimentation, and stratigraphical completeness', *Nature*.

Varèse, Edgar(1984) *Ecuatorial*, including Mayan prayer translated in programme note, Royal Festival Hall. The performance included Jeanne Loriod and Cynthia Miller playing Ondes Martenots.

Waddington, C.H. (ed.)(1968, 1970, 1972) *Towards a Theoretical Biology*: Vol. 1 *Prolegomena*; Vol. 3 *Drafts*; and Vol. 4 *Essays*, Edinburgh and Chicago. Includes work from Waddington, Lewis Wolpert and Christopher Zeeman.

Walls, D.F. (1983) 'Squeezed states of light, Hamilton', New Zealand.

Whalley, E., and J. Poirier (1984) 'Ices in the Solar System', Ottawa and Paris.

Whitney, H. (1955) 'On singularities of mappings of Euclidean spaces I. Mappings of the plane into the plane', *Ann. Math. 2*.

Williams, William Carlos (1951) *Autobiography*, New York.

Wilson, Kenneth (1982) various discussions of his application of particle fields theory to analytical solutions of thermodynamic lattice problems and phase shifts, e.g. *Nature*.

Witkin, Herman A. (1959) *The Perception of the Upright*, San Francisco.

Wordsworth, William (1827) Sonnet XLIV.

Zeeman, E.C. (1977) *Catastrophe Theory, Selected Papers 1972–77*, Massachusetts.

Zeeman, E.C. (1979) 'A Geometrical Model of Ideologies in Transformations', included in *Mathematical Approaches to Cultural Change*.

Zeeman, E.C. (1960) *Unknotting Sphere in Five Dimensions, Bulletin of the American Mathematical Society*.

Zeldovich, Ya. B. with J. Einasto and S.F. Shandarin (1982) 'Giant voids in the Universe', *Nature*.

Dispossession & Cure Resources and Notes list.

Dirty Dog: Virginia Woolf (1931) *The Waves*.
The art referred to is exhibited at Knightsbridge Crown Court.

Accounts

An article, now lost, giving a floral chemical analysis of perfumes
used by heads of state.
C.T.J. Dodson and T. Poston (1977) *Tensor Geometry, The Geometric
Viewpoint and its uses*, London and Belmont, California.

Convalescence

Richard Bauman, *Verbal Art as Performance*.
Ruth Benedict, *Patterns of Culture*.
John Bellany in conversation on television, March 1989.
Jack Bilbo (1945) *Pablo Picasso: Thirty Important Paintings from 1904 to
1943*, London.
William Blake, *Notebook*, N36–N39.
Elizabeth Barrett Browning Elizabeth Berridge (ed.) (1974) "A Curse for a
Nation", 1856, and from her Diary beginning 4th June 1831.
Burton, W. Kates, G.F. White (1978) *The Environment as Hazard*.
Cyril Connolly, Comment, *Horizon*, January 1940.
Jacopo Coppi, *Invention of Gun Powder*, one of the painting in the
Studiolo of Francesco I de' Medici in the Palazzo Vecchio,
Florence, c.1568-75.
Marguerite Duras (1985) *Le Douleur*.
Nigel Franks (1989) *The Swarms of Complexity*, reported by Matt
Nicholson.
Stephen Spender (1989) *Waiting for the bombers*.
Adrian Stokes (1959) *Art and Science, A Study of Alberti, Piero della
Francesca, and Giogione*, London.

Thomas Traherne, 'On News', 'Desire', 'Nature', and 'Innocence'. *Journal of the Warburg and Courtauld Institutes*, Volume 44, 1981.
Marcus Weisen (1987) 'Oxford unseen', *The British Journal of Visual Impairment*, Volume 1, Spring.

Work Consciousness Commodity: Three Kinds of Perception

Simone de Beauvoir (1984) *Adieux*, trans. Patrick O'Brian, New York.
Phil Drabble (1969) *Badgers at my window*, London.
Allen Fisher (1985–6.) an unpublished text discussing the work of Joseph Beuys.
Peter Hardy, *A Lifetime of Badgers*, Newton Abbot, London.
Richard Hayman (1986) *Writing Against, A Biography of Sartre*, London.
Frederick Jameson (1961) *Sartre: The Origins of a Style*, New Haven.
Richard Perry (1978) *Wildlife in Britain and Ireland*, London.
Sartre by Himself (1978) trans. Richard Seaver, New York.

Disposession and Cure

Peter Brook interviewed in *Time*, 1991.
Filippo Brunelleschi, The Pazzi Chapel.
Ted Cohen and Paul Guyer (eds.)(1982) *Essays in Kant's Aesthetics*, Chicago and London.
Dante, *The Divine Comedy, Paradiso*, the end of Canto 33.
Gilles Deleuze (1963, 1984) *Kant's Critical Philosophy, The Doctrine of the Faculties*, trans. Hugh Tomlinson and Barbara Habberjam, Minneapolis.
Domenico di Michel, fresco in S.Maria Fiore.
The Riddles from The Exeter Book, no.15, translated by John Porter, Market Drayton, 1978.
E.H. Gombrich (1979) *The Sense of Order, A study on the psychology of decorative art*, London.
Jasper Johns (1973) interviewed in *Art News*, March.

Immanuel Kant (1960) *Observations on the Feeling of the Beautiful and Sublime*, trans. John T. Goldthwait, California.

Immanuel Kant (1928, 1952) *Critique of (Aesthetic) Judgement*, trans. James Creed Meredith.

Benoit B. Mandelbröt (1977) *FRACTALS, Form, Chance, and Dimension*, San Francisco.

Martin Pawley (1990) *Eva Jiricna, Design in Exile*, London.

Joesph Paxton, Design for the Crystal Palace, 1851, redesigned for Sydenham Hill, 1852.

George Rhee, Las Cruces, New Mexico, reported measurement of the disputed Hubble constant, *Nature* 21.3.91.

Jean-Paul Sartre (1976) *Critique of Dialectical Reason*, vol.1, *Theory of Practical Ensembles*, trans. Alan Sheridan Smith, London.

Cyril Stanley Smith (1981) *A Search for Structure, Selected Essays on Science, Art and History*, MIT, Cambridge, Mass.

Springboard of Bristol, the stairs at Josephs in London, 1988, designed for Eva Jiricna.

Stratagene, 1991, Cambridge, Details on 'in style' cloning and designer genes.

The cover for *Fizz* included an eighteen century engraving by R.Scott proposed as the 'Exterior of the Ark' which is juxtaposed to Allen Fisher's photograph of the mill at Lugg Meadows, Hereford. The frontispiece included the following:

"Do not in your relations with your left-hand neighbour what annoys you if done at your right, nor in your relations to your right-hand neighbour what annoys you if done at your left. This is called having the compass and T-square of process." Tseng's comments on Confucius' *Ta Hsio, The Great Digest*, Ezra Pound's 1928 translation.

Printed in the United States
20086LVS00005B/1-39

9 781844 710348